What the Hell ?

A Biblical Truth About Hell

AFOLABI EHIKIOYA

Copyright © 2023 Afolabi Ehikioya.
Second Edition

All rights reserved. No part of this book may be reproduced, stored, or transmitted by any means—whether auditory, graphic, mechanical, or electronic—without written permission of both publisher and author, except in the case of brief excerpts used in critical articles and reviews. Unauthorized reproduction of any part of this work is illegal and is punishable by law.

Unless otherwise indicated, all scriptures are from the King James Version.

ISBN: 979-8-89031-309-6 (sc)
ISBN: 979-8-89031-310-2 (hc)
ISBN: 979-8-89031-311-9 (e)

Because of the dynamic nature of the Internet, any web addresses or links contained in this book may have changed since publication and may no longer be valid. The views expressed in this work are solely those of the author and do not necessarily reflect the views of the publisher, and the publisher hereby disclaims any responsibility for them.

One Galleria Blvd., Suite 1900, Metairie, LA 70001
(504) 702-6708
1-888-421-2397

This book is dedicated to my King Christ Jesus, my family, my father in the Lord, to all truth lovers and lovers of the gospel who are in search of the good word of God, and to those who desire the real purpose of their lives through the gospel.

"When a man stops learning, he stops growing."
"You are a product of what you know."

—Afolabi. E

Special thanks to my beautiful wife who endured through my long hours of writing, and all who dutifully contributed to the project of this book such as Shonie Ehikioya, Abitha Ibe, Shahilia Ehikioya, and Tessamay McKenzie.

CONTENTS

1. **The Myths of Hell** 1
   Islam and Hell 7
   Buddhism and Hell 10

2. **What is Hell?** 13
   Is hell the destination of the wicked? 13

3. **Where is Hell?** 27

4. **Wages and Gifts** 33

5. **Immortality of the Soul!** 39
   Man, Soul, and the Dust 40
   The Soul and the Creature 42
   No Immortality Without a Resurrection 50
   Souls of The Slain Crying Out? 54

6. **Lazarus and the Rich Man** 58
   Why in Parable? 61
   The Rich Man 64
   The Gate, The Sores, and The Dogs 66
   Crumbs 67
   Dogs 68
   The Beggar 71
   The Bosom 73

    Table 77
    The Dip of Cool Water 78
    The Great Gulf 80
    The Five Brethren 85

7. **What is the Gate of Hell?** 88

8. **The Dead is Dead** 98

9. **The Weeping and Gnashing of Teeth** 103

1

The Myths of Hell

"There has been a struggle among humanity to understand, identify, and relate with the doctrine and the existence of hell. While some consider it a weird topic of discussion, the temptation to unravel this mystery remains undeniable. The subject of hell remains a mystery to be resolved among humanity with those who care to know the truth of the word of God.

This age-old teaching and doctrine concerning "hell" is all based on a revelation from God and the infallible proof of the scriptures. Only those whom the Lord chooses to give this understanding could attain by the revelation of that which God Himself could give to them as He did for Peter in the days of Jesus Christ. *"And Jesus answered and said unto him, 'Blessed art thou, Simon Barjona: for flesh and blood hath not revealed it unto thee, but my Father which is in heaven'" (Matthew 16:17).*

Without God giving man an insight to the depth of the truth, what that man is going to rely on will be nothing else than fables and old folk tales.

This subject of hell has passed through many decades and centuries of civilization and state religious beliefs without a clear interpretation of what the so-called hell could mean. Because they sought it not by

God's revelation but by human standards of learning, which leads to nothing but death, *". . . for the letter killeth, but the spirit giveth life"* (2 Corinthians 3:6).

No one by the basis of human enlightenment can attain the revelation of the truth. For truth comes only by Christ, or by God the Father. Christ says, *"I am the way, the truth, and the life" (John 14:6).*

Unfortunately, men of human mind have tried to explain away the reality of hell, but only to become enslaved to the same, a system of darkness that uses the tools of fear rather than truth to command the loyalty of unsuspecting men and women that are hungry for the truth of the word of God.

We realize that the law of retributive justice is accorded to all races, people, tongues, and nations, and it is our common legacy from the time of the fall in the Garden of Eden until the present for everyone to continually stand in fear of the unknown.

When man fell, he was exposed to all types of sin in such a fashion that eluded him of the peace he should have had when he encountered God. From that time on, man was no longer able to accentuate the presence of God as they freely did before the fall took place.

Apostle Paul stated, how that it is a fearful thing to fall into the hands of the living God. Hebrews 10:3 *says, "It is a fearful thing to fall into the hands of the living God."* Fleeing from the presence of an angry God, and not knowing where nor how vengeance would strike, had men living in fear of eternal judgment all their lives. Adam's statement in the Garden of Eden, in response to God's question, when Adam and Eve failed God in adhering to God's commandment was, "I heard thy voice, and I was afraid." *"And he said, 'I heard thy voice in the garden, and I was afraid, because I was naked; and I hid myself'" (Genesis 3:10).* Man today is still in search of that refuge they once had from God, or at least a kingdom that could shield them from the barrage of hell.

The idea of an ever-burning hell has frightened countless millions, and this fear has driven many souls to all sorts of beliefs that are baseless.

This fear is no more an illusion. The thought has become so real that what really happens to the wicked after death becomes an unavoidable question. Are we all doomed to hell? Is the human "soul" waiting to roast in "torment" forever? These and other questions in relation to hell are what this book is designed to help interested readers to understand.

If hell exists, will the wicked go there? Where is it, what is it, and if it does exist, when do individuals get there? These unresolved questions keep ringing back and forth in the heart of all liberal-minded persons. Can hell be a burning pit of no return? Could there be a possible explanation that might vary from the popular church dogma?

Then also come the questions about the resurrection of the dead, the parable of Lazarus and the rich man, the many popular beliefs about the fate of unrepentant sinners, and the immortality of the soul. Such questions as, does the soul move out alive while the host is dead? All these mind-boggling questions about gender confusion remain as issues that the Bible must answer. So, what would be the Bible's answers to these questions with the intent to understand what hell is?

Many individuals have always looked upon religion to be very primitive, uncultured, and untested. So, they spent most of their life seeking its source and origins to no avail. Amid all these uncertainties, there has been one point of reconciliation that cannot be ignored. That is, the point that man must make peace with God in order to evade His wrath over the displeasure of man's conduct and lifestyle towards Him.

The desire to live a fulfilled life free from guilt and restitution has made it clear that men cannot live alone without God, nor could men live outside of God. For men not only had to be at peace with God, but they needed to be at peace with themselves if they must live in the eternal presence of their maker, their creator, and God the Almighty. This reality will be impossible without the quickening and the favor of God Himself upon mankind.

In Ephesians 2:1, the Bible says, "... *you hath he quickened, who were dead in trespasses and sins,*" intently establishing the understanding that none of the Adamic offspring with the death penalty over their lives can assist in their own reconciliation, restoration, or resurrection.

For instance, there is a narration that when a fish is taken out of water, it struggles, and if care is not taken, the fish dies. When creatures are taken away from the presence of air that they breathe, they struggle and die, and so are men when taken away from the presence of God, they struggle with their spirituality and ultimately die. Proving that man cannot self-sustain himself outside of God, any more can any creature survive outside their intended habitation.

In the bid for man to find his way back to God, his maker, man took his first faltering and fearful steps toward God, by presenting God with a sacrifice. Abel offered a firstling of a lamb sacrifice, while Cain brought the fruit of the ground for a sacrifice. God accepted the sacrifice of Abel but, that of Cain, He rejected. Unfortunately, Abel who would have led by example on how to appease God over a failed creation, was brutally killed by Cain.

When men could have had a teacher of faith, a priest, such as Abel—one who could teach, instruct, and intercede on behalf of fellow mankind—Cain, his only brother, forcefully took away that opportunity. This left God no choice, but to set in place the judgment of retribution on the earth. This judgment set the precedence for all other judgments that are to follow until the present.

However, his judgment granted him the Marks of Grace, which God placed upon him, not allowing anyone who finds him to slay him, regardless of his crime against creation and humanity. Since then, man has based their system of belief on the act of sin and ruthlessness, ignoring the loving kindness of God.

This understanding causes many to live in fear, rather than faith in the living God who leadeth all, forgiveth all, and is full of mercy and compassion for all. To this day, man has magnified the judgment of God rather than the mercy of his grace to the detriment of their own selves. *"For he shall have judgment without mercy, that hath shewed no mercy; and mercy rejoiceth against judgment" (James 2:13).*

From thence, men lived in fear of the unknown, and of uncertainty, but God never left us without a witness and comfort of hope. *"The fear of the LORD is a fountain of life, to depart from the snares of death" (Proverbs 14:27). "The fear of man bringeth a snare: but whoso putteth his trust into the LORD shall be safe" (Proverbs 29:25).*

Man's fear of the wrath of God and his dread of divine retribution played right into the hands of many priests of the world's early religions. They immediately recognized the power it offered to those who were wise enough to exploit it for their own gain. They used this fear factor to manipulate unsuspecting, faithful, and unstable souls to their personal advantage.

So out of man's need for peace with his God, he became a slave of inherited fear, which unnumberable self-acclaimed priests around the world by false religions have taken advantage of and exploited to their personal benefit. *"While they promise them liberty, they themselves are the servants of corruption: for of whom a man is overcome, of the same is he brought in" (2 Peter 2:19).*

Fear repeatedly became a vital tool that fell into the hands of insidious mighty men, underhanded priests, and sly spiritual leaders, who discovered the potential of such powers. These rose quickly, without hesitation, nor the fear of God, went ahead to harness, harass, and intimidate men even unto death, damning the repercussions thereon.

This element of fear that God has not given to any of His creation, became a plague to the church and early parishioners. Fear which should have been used to honor God, to reverence Him, and to worship Him, is rather used to intimidate and exploit unknowledgeable souls, from the inception of life, till the hours of death, beginning at birth, even extending into eternity. Man, from the fall at the Garden of Eden, has remained in bondage of this callous act till this day.

These men turned the fear of hell into doctrines of eternal damnation and everlasting punishment contrary to God's purpose for humanity. These men of old, ungodly men took this principle and made it into doctrines for organized state religion to use for the purpose of holding the masses in spiritual slavery. Thus, man was bound in terror and strict obedience to the manipulation of the state-dominated religionist. And so began a travesty that will be revealed on the judgment day as one of the world's greatest frauds by spiritual con strategists.

In light of this understanding, it didn't matter what sort of leaders these men were, or what denomination they represented. It will be important to see how these various religious sects set their strongholds on their belief as facts to the proof of this doctrine that they and many have labeled HELL. The Latin world and the papal system of religion beginning from around the 4th century AD sought to combine their beliefs with pagan rites in establishing various forms of hells to validate their message of mind control by their doctrine of hell, which by the standard of the Bible does not hold the same validity in accordance with the Bible truth contained in the sixty-six books of God's word.

Many in the Latin world believe and claim that hell, which is *infernus* in Latin, is divided into three segments. However, this is something to investigate in comparison to the word of God, as their belief of hell may not hold with God's truth altogether. These three segments are limbo of children, limbo of fathers, and purgatory.

Limbo of the Children. In Latin is *limbus parvulorum*. In referring to those who may have died in their original sin, that is sins of early ages, without personal mortal sin, may enjoy natural stress without the agony of pain. For those who might not know, original sin, is also known as ancestral sin, a form of sin religionists believe applies to someone who may have inherited such sins from Adam's fallen nature, which, if not been checked and restricted can become a part of some person's life, such sins as disobedience, lust, greed and so on. Like David said in his prayers, *"Behold, I was shapen in iniquity; and in sin did my mother conceive me"* (*Psalms 51:5*).

Limbo of the Fathers. In Latin is *limbus partum,* as the name implies, is when the souls of the Old Testament saints who died before the coming of Christ awaited their clearance to enter into heaven. Some claimed this to be "Abraham's bosom." A claim which some say is blissful without the sensation of pain, a limbo which they also believe is currently vacant. Claiming its vacancy must be because the saints of old are supposed to be presently alive somewhere in the heavens, or else the claimed theory would be fallible.

Purgatory. The claim that the righteous who die in venial sin, or should we say still owe a debt of temporal punishment for sin they committed in this life, are cleansed by suffering in purgatory before their admission to heaven.

What is not quite clear in all these claims is how to validate these understanding in reference to the Word of God, the Holy Bible.

ISLAM AND HELL

Now, whether you are Muslim, Christian, Buddhist, Hindu, or a pagan, truth will always remain as truth, no matter anyone's personal belief. Especially with a subject of hell like this that is universal. The subject of this matter should not be treated less than it deserves when compared to other universal subjects, such as life, death, the resurrection, the sovereignty of God, and end-time rewards, among others. In other words, the topic, hell, should carry the same weight or volume of truth across the board. From a standpoint of a believer in the word of God, it is expedient that hell as a subject should have to its credit a universal truth that everybody can agree upon, no matter who they are or where they come from.

In the Western world, many believe that hell is a place of eternal fire, sulfur, and smoke; where the soul of the unrepentant dead is judged permanently throughout eternity and without a means of escape—ever. Amazing, anyone would say. That in spite of all of these understanding, some would try living their lives free of these doctrinal heresies or try to avoid going there, but no. They still until today walk in blindness.

The religion of Islam also developed their views of hell. Just as Christians believe in hell, so do the Muslims. They portray the picture of hell as we should expect a religious people to imagine hell in their religious mind. They sculptured hell as a place, where anyone found short of expectation could face judgment for all their wrongdoings, for all eternity.

The Muslims believe that when a person dies, whether he or she be righteous or evil as an individual, they all remain in the grave until the last day. However, while in the grave, it is said that those who may have failed their God while alive will be bound for hell which they call "Jahannam," a place where they would experience some level of suffering and pain. *"Surely, those who disbelieve and did wrong; God will not forgive them, nor will He guide them to any way except the way of Hell, to dwell therein forever"* (Quran 4:168–169).

Those who did virtuous deeds while alive, though they remain in the grave, they would experience peace being bound for paradise. In Islam, hell is real, and it is a place for those who may have received or heard the truth and blatantly reject it. *"And whosoever disobeys God and His Messenger, then surely, for him is the fire of Hell, he shall dwell therein forever"* (Quran 72:23).

"Surely, the gates of Heaven will not be opened for those who deny Our revelations and treat them with arrogance; their admission into paradise will be as impossible as the passing of a camel through the eye of a needle. That is how We shall reward the criminals. Hell shall be their bed and flames shall be their covering. That is how We shall reward the wrongdoers" (Quran 7:40–41).

The Quran is very loud about the description of hell, to the point where it is impossible for any practicing Muslim to fail in knowing and acknowledging the reality of hell. In the Quran, there are numerous names for hell such as *Jahannam*: Deep pit, *Jahīm*: A blazing fire, *Saʿīr*: Kindled fire, *Hāwīya:* Deep place, and *Ḥuṭama*: meaning Debris.

The Muslims believe that hell is divided into seven levels, not seven segments. Seven levels deep, it is said to be so deep that if a piece of rock were to be dropped into it, it would take seventy years for that piece of rock to hit the bottom of hell. It is well established that the gravity of one's iniquity will determine the severity of suffering and the level or depth such one will land in hell, thereby stating everybody doesn't suffer the same degree of pain, suffering, or anguish in hell. Therefore, everyone who goes to hell must suffer both spiritually and physically regardless. A place of torment of flaming fire. *"Surely, God has cursed the disbelievers, and has prepared for them a flaming Fire wherein they will abide forever" (Quran 33:64).*

In hell, the Quran tells us that there is some kind of food made available to those in it, from the tree called *Zaqum*. This tree is said to be rooted at the bottom of hell itself, in the lowest parts of hell and its branches are described to resemble the head and horns of devils. *"Then indeed you, O those astray (who are) deniers, will be eating from trees of zaqūm and filling with it your bellies, and drinking on top of it from scalding water, and will drink as the drinking of thirsty camels. That is their hospitality on the Day of Recompense" (Quran 56:51–56).*

"Is Paradise better as an abode or the tree of zaqūm? Indeed, we have made it a torment for the wrongdoers. Indeed, it is a tree issuing from the bottom of the Hellfire, its emerging fruit as if it was the heads of the devils. And, indeed, they will eat from it and fill with it their bellies. Then, indeed, they will have after it a mixture of scalding water. Then, indeed, their return will be to the Hellfire" (Quran 37:62–68).

The taste of the food from this tree is bitter and will only add more pain to those who eat from it, *"Indeed, the tree of zaqūm is food for the sinful, like murky oil, it boils within bellies, like the boiling of scalding water" (Quran 44:43–46).*

"No food will there be for them except from a bitter, thorny plant which neither nourishes nor avails against hunger" (Quran 88:6–7).

BUDDHISM AND HELL

Just like the Muslim religion, the Chinese Buddhists also have an overly complex theology concerning the abode of the wicked dead. Though not thoroughly defined, because of the many planes, it is understood that in Buddhism there are over thirty such planes. There is the Brahma plane, Beva plane, Gaki plane, Asura plane, Peta plane, Thiracchana plane, and the Niraya plane, just to mention a few. It is based on whatever the plane is, that determines what hell we are likely to talk about in the Buddhist faith. It is quite complex to give a proper narration about the subject of hell in the Buddhist religion, however, the most popular or rather, the most common name for hell is known as Narakas. While some advocate that there is no literal hell, others believe that when an individual is at their worst or lowest level in life, they are just as much in hell, and if things are going well, then it must mean such individuals are experiencing heaven.

Some believe the hell of the Buddhist faith has as many as over 130 regions. Some of these infernal regions are said to be under the earth and consist of three earths—prisons of hell, the lowest being a burning hell with iron walls, while the other is considered as ice-cooling hell.

It may also come as a surprise to our readers that there is a general agreement among the day's religion and their ancient counterparts as to their exact views on this subject, to be the place or abode of the wicked dead.

There is also widespread disagreement on the gates of hell. The size of the gates, their shape, the number of entrances, and their locations have never been determined with any pledge of agreement, unlike the Muslims, who distinctively establish in their doctrine that there are seven gates of hell according to their religion.

The various estimates concerning the size of hell is also marked by inconsistency in Chinese Buddhism. However, it had been calculated that their belief of the size of hell was an estimated area of about 40,000 square miles, which would be somewhat smaller than New York State.

While another writer, whom we cannot authenticate, estimates hell to be 216,000 times larger than Earth. A fact that cannot be substantiated. Many scholars of distinct knowledge divided hell into seven regions or compartments in order to buttress their claims. No matter what some may advocate on this subject, only one fact stands out, and that is, their claim that hell is a place that is constantly on fire, with an endless inferno. A fact that is not supported by the word of God, which we are going to review as we go further in this study.

We are made to see that humanity has been a victim of an age-old conspiracy with spiritual intimidation and discrepancies, subdued by fears and held in bondage by spiritual ignorance.

Today, man has finally awakened out of that spiritual ignorance and slumber and have chosen not to remain silent, but seek the truth on this age-old doctrine of hell that has terrorized the church and the world at large for centuries. For this cause, many boldly, without fear or recourse now dare to question, demanding answers concerning the true meaning or interpretation of hell. Man, relentlessly sought to break these chains that have kept him bound these many centuries. Everywhere, this age-old position of the church on the doctrine has been a challenge. At last, men now dare to ask questions and demand answers.

Individuals no longer blindly believe their teachers, though the terror of hell still holds them bound in the agony of fear. They are plainly asking, Is this doctrine true? Are there really any answers? Where can one go or look to find answers? In what can we trust? The answers only rest in the infallible truth of the Holy Book, the Bible, which is one of the authorities of truth given to humanity.

WHAT THE HELL?

Have you looked into your Bible for the answer? Do you know what the Bible has to say concerning "divine retribution" and the "doctrines of hell"?

For man to be without excuse, it becomes obligatory to find the truth of this age-old mystery and unravel all myths, superstitions, and fables, to bring peace and rest in all of our hearts as we make ourselves ready to read this expository book on hell.

2

What is Hell?

IS HELL THE DESTINATION OF THE WICKED?

Regardless of what anyone chooses to believe about hell, over the years, there are many acclaimed fables of the experience of hell. Just as we've seen from the previous title, 'the myths of hell,' some individuals have proclaimed they've seen hell literally. Some say they were carried or transcended into heaven where they had the opportunity of seeing the abode of hell burning with sulfur and brimstone, even the gates of heaven or the Kingdom, the luxury or leisure of it, and somehow, were asked to return back to this earth and its evil so as to be a witness to the rest of humanity. Those who make these claims are sometimes coma survivors, or those who claimed they actually died for days or weeks, but our good Lord sent them back. How true or credible these testimonies are, is yet to be assessed or vetted.

These men and women who proclaimed witnessing hell and its fury while they were bodily dead, said they saw men and women popping and frying in hell, being tormented; souls living in severe pain, others screaming for help, thirsty to death, with no mercy shown to them. Among others, are those who are said to live as villains in hell as taskmasters or hell porters. And so goes on many more of these tales that's ravaged the human mind. What is so unfortunate about these claims is that these reports are practically in opposition to God and His word. All of these assertions are in total violation of the scriptures, especially as it is written in the book of Ecclesiastes 9:5–6,10, *"For the living know that they shall die: but the dead know not anything, neither have they any more a reward; for the memory of them is forgotten. Also their love, and their hatred, and their envy, is now perished; neither have they any more a portion forever in anything that is done under the sun . . . Whatsoever thy hand findeth to do, do it with thy might; for there is no work, nor device, nor knowledge, nor wisdom, in the grave, whither thou goest."*

Now, if there be *"no work, nor device, nor knowledge, nor wisdom, in the grave, whither thou goest,"* then the question remains, with what knowledge will they who would be in hell realize their faults, guilt, sins, or transgressions? How would they know for what cause, or purpose they are being tormented for, days and nights on end? This is a question that we all must ask ourselves, and those believing in the theory of torment and torture in hell, whether they be Christians, Muslims, Hindus, Buddhists, or pagans.

Contrary to the popular belief and understanding that hell may be a "last days" event, or even the final destination for the wicked, unworthy, unrighteous, and sinners, how else would we then justify the scripture written in Revelation 20:12–14? *"And I saw the dead, small and great, stand before God; and the books were opened: and another book was opened, which is the book of life: and the dead were judged out of those things which were written in them, according to their works. And the sea gave up the dead which were in it; and death and hell delivered up the dead which were in them: and they were judged every man according to their works. And death and hell were cast into the lake of fire. This is the second death.* For the Bible clearly spoke out, loud and clear, saying, *"For the wages of sin is death"*(Romans 6:23).

Meaning, death is the final destination of the unrighteous dead. Not a populated hell of the tormented, as many have believed or as some would want the Bible to sound to their hearing, and advantage of their sense of oppression, whereby they oppressed and deceived a vast majority of persons in the name of religion and not the various levels associated with hell.

Another school of thought that we must consider is, if hell is the final destination of the wicked, why would God turn around and bring the unrighteous dead from the same hell the world claimed as the judgment place of the wicked? How is this understanding even justified in reasoning? "*. . . death and hell delivered up the dead which were in them: and they were judged every man according to their works.*" Meaning there is still going to be judgment after men have been to and through hell. So the question that should be boggling our minds now should be, "What is hell?" Or even better, the question we should be asking ourselves is, the word "hell"—is it even found in the Bible exactly as it is meant to sound or referred to at all? Again, even if it were to be written in our Bible, is the word "hell" translated properly, and does it mean what the secular world refers it to be? Do you know that most biblical translations don't even contain the word "hell" even a single time?

The King James Bible, which is widely considered to be one of the most accurate translations, and most widely used texts among the Christian faith contains fifty-four occurrences of the word hell. Other translations, like the New International Version (NIV), barely have hell mentioned in it, and even in some passages, the word hell was omitted. For example, the Revised Standard Version (RSV) Bible does not contain the word hell at all but rather maintained the original Hebrew word translated into hell, which is *Sheol* in the Old Testament, and in the New Testament, the Greek word, *Hades*.

It will be interesting at this point to look at some vital words mostly used in the Bible, even with their translations and their occurrences. Words such as "sin" was mentioned over six hundred times, "kingdom," mentioned over seven hundred times, "evil," over five hundred times, "heaven," over six hundred times, "Father," over 1,600 times, "soul," almost five hundred times, "death," five hundred times, and "judgment," mentioned over 1,250 times.

With all that has been stated and the number of times they were mentioned, whether it be heaven, sin, or death, hell is only known to be mentioned just fifty-four times in comparison to other frequently used words. Hell, being a vital part of the judgment of God should have been mentioned far more than any aspect of the reward of the wicked than is given credence.

With hell known to be a vital part of sin, judgment, and death, or rather the end result of sinners, it should get more attention in the word of God just as poverty, wealth, and money get talked about over two thousand times and over.

The supported belief of hell is not a secret or a mystery to any who is an interested convert of the faith. Because it is assumed that God is actually going to barbecue a countless number of sinners in the pit of hell, allowing them to permanently agonize for all of eternity, it would be easy to believe that hell should command a greater authority in the scriptures than all the aforementioned subjects listed above. Much more than money that is referenced 2,699 times in the Bible, or even heaven that is spoken of over six hundred times.

As a good believer or a good student of the Bible, it will be noteworthy to know what the true translation of this word and subject called hell really means. The word hell, though an English word, is translated from the Hebrew word Sheol, and the Greek word Hades.

There are nearly seven different words used in reference to hell, using the King James Version as a base for our understanding. Most of the confusion around hell starts with translation error. Hell is used as **1) Sheol, 2) Hades, 3) Gehenna, 4) Tartarus, 5) Pit, 6) Lake of Fire, and 7. Grave.**

1. Sheol (H7585) שְׁאוֹל she'ôl,
From H7592; Hades or the world of the dead (as if a subterranean retreat), including its accessories and inmates: – grave, hell, pit.

2. Hades (G86) ᾅδης
Hades From G1 (as a negative particle) and G1492; properly unseen, that is, "Hades" or the place (state) of departed souls: – grave, hell.

3. Gehenna (G1067) γέεννα geenna, gheh'-en-nah.
Of Hebrew origin ([H1516] and [H2011]); valley of (the son of) Hinnom; gehenna (or Ge-Hinnom), a valley of Jerusalem

4. Tartarus (G5020) Ταρταρόω, tartaroō, tar-tar-o'-o
From Τάρταρος Tartaros (the deepest abyss of Hades); to incarcerate in eternal torment: – cast down to hell.

You'll notice that NONE of the four words mentioned above out of the seven actually translated into hell. The closest would be Hades, which is derived from Greek mythology and is never actually translated to "hell" in academically accepted translations. Sheol and Hades are both always translated as "death," or "the grave," in various Bible texts and other more accurate translations. In other words, "hell" is NOT actually a proper translation in the Bible as many would like it to sound.

A claim like this warrants a worthy defense, and that's why we are going to possibly look at every single time the word "hell" is used in the Bible as much as possible or if at all necessary. Because Sheol, Hades, Gehenna, and Tartarus are actually not English words like Pit, Lake of Fire, and Grave that are used to symbolize hell in the scriptures. These are self-explanatory, after considering the meaning of the four non-English words noted in the previous paragraphs. We will discuss this understanding in detail later in this book.

The name Gehenna is known in the Old Testament as a dark place where children were being sacrificed to a pagan God called Molech in the valley of Hinnom. *"Moreover, he burnt incense in the valley of the son of Hinnom, and burnt his children in the fire, after the abominations of the heathen whom the LORD had cast out before the children of Israel"* (*2 Chronicles 28:3*).

With the consciousness of the doctrine of hell and the claim that it is a place burning with fire, was a no in the sight of the almighty God. When Manasseh, the son of Hezekiah chose to raise altars to Baalim to burn his children, this was against God. Read 2 Chronicles 33:1–6: *"Manasseh was twelve years old when he began to reign, and he reigned fifty and five years in Jerusalem. But did that which was evil in the sight of the LORD, like unto the abominations of the heathen, whom the LORD had cast out before the children of Israel. For he built again the high places which Hezekiah his father had broken down, and he reared up altars for Baalim, and made groves, and worshipped all the host of heaven, and served them. Also he built altars in the house of the LORD, whereof the LORD had said, In Jerusalem shall my name be forever. And he built altars for all the host of heaven in the two courts of the house of the LORD. And he caused his children to pass through the fire in the valley of the son of Hinnom: also, he observed times, and used enchantments, and used witchcraft, and dealt with a familiar spirit, and with wizards: he wrought much evil in the sight of the LORD, to provoke him to anger."*

Now, this is a scripture that proves God's disapproval, which is too good to be ignored concerning the concept of God burning men with fire as a state of judgment or a reward for their evildoing on earth on the last day. It is amazing that this narration of barbecuing souls in a fearsome inferno was never a thought in God's mind as many religious bigots profess to claim. *"And they built the high places of Baal, which are in the valley of the son of Hinnom, to cause their sons and their daughters to pass through the fire unto Molech; which I commanded them not, neither came it into my mind, that they should do this abomination, to cause Judah to sin"* (*Jeremiah 32:35*).

The presence of such wickedness in this valley caused God to curse the valley with a bitter curse for various, yet obvious reasons. First of all, because God did not design humanity to be burned by fire as a means of punishment, how much more as a sacrifice. *"For the children of Judah have done evil in my sight, saith the LORD: they have set their abominations in the house which is called by my name, to pollute it. And they have built the high places of Tophet, which is in the valley of the son of Hinnom, to burn their sons and their daughters in the fire; which I commanded them not, neither came it into my heart. Therefore, behold, the days come, saith the LORD, that it shall no more be called Tophet, nor the valley of the son of Hinnom, but the valley of slaughter: for they shall bury in Tophet, till there be no place. And the carcasses of this people shall be meat for the fowls of the heaven, and for the beasts of the earth; and none shall fray them away. Then will I cause to cease from the cities of Judah, and from the streets of Jerusalem, the voice of mirth, and the voice of gladness, the voice of the bridegroom, and the voice of the bride: for the land shall be desolate"* (Jeremiah 7:30–34).

For God commanded Moses to speak against such heinous, notorious, and barbaric act, saying, "*. . . thou shalt not let any of thy seed pass through the fire to Molech, neither shalt thou profane the name of thy God: I am the LORD*" (Leviticus 18:21).

"*And the LORD spake unto Moses, saying, Again, thou shalt say to the children of Israel, Whosoever he be of the children of Israel, or of the strangers that sojourn in Israel, that giveth any of his seed unto Molech; he shall surely be put to death: the people of the land shall stone him with stones. And I will set my face against that man and will cut him off from among his people; because he hath given of his seed unto Molech, to defile my sanctuary, and to profane my holy name. And if the people of the land do any ways hide their eyes from the man, when he giveth of his seed unto Molech, and kill him not: Then I will set my face against that man, and against his family, and will cut him off, and all that go a whoring after him, to commit whoredom with Molech, from among their people" (Leviticus 20:1–5).*

Now, if God is displeased with such a sacrifice of people being burnt with fire, why would Christ then come on earth to establish a judgment by burning, that has no eternal consequences? That is why this valley, for what it is known for, a place of fiery torment and sacrifices to honor their pagan gods, was burned down by King Josiah, thereby letting the valley remain as a refuse and garbage dump till this day.

No one goes to the grave, or the Hebrew Sheol (hell), that can have any more a portion of anything done under the sun, as the Bible says, nor do they have any memory of any sort—so, the question remains, by what means do they function or operate in hell? If they cannot work, neither do they have any form of knowledge in them, how are they able to express the pain or agony from this place of torment?

It might be questionable how these self-acclaimed, transcending individuals have the knowledge of what they see and remember what hell looks like, if they claimed they died literally. Well, it will be my guess that someone is playing on the intelligence of an unsuspecting audience who knows no better.

Hell, as it does sound, will lose its fury if this luxury of knowledge and this ever-existent life dwell with it. For the Bible says, *"Let no man deceive you, whatsoever ye do now today, do all in the name of the Lord Jesus Christ" (Colossians 3:17).* If a man has not successfully lived the life he beholds, how does he plan to live a life well, which he hath not seen?

As we have seen, many have made much effort to seek the size of hell, and probably establish a doctrine based upon the apparent subject, but the question that must be answered, or taken into consideration is, what is hell?

The word "hell," which is translated from a Hebrew word called "Sheol" and the Greek language called "Hades" or Gehenna, has been translated most unfortunately to suit what an individual claim they feel or assume what hell is or rather what they wish hell should be.

Based on various versions of the English Bible, we shall see that not one particular translation can boast a proper or concise transcription of the four-letter word hell.

The King James Version maintained the use of hell when it speaks in reference to the wicked, but when it applies to the righteous, it refers to them as going down to the grave (Sheol in other words). The same scripture that is used as Sheol, is interpreted as grave to the righteous, and hell to the wicked. Let us see the views of this subject as it is laid out in various passages of the Bible.

In the King James Version, Psalms 9:17 speaks of the wicked as hell material. *"The wicked shall be turned into hell, and all the nations that forget God."* However, in the Amplified Bible (AMP), we see differently. Psalms 9:17 (AMP): *"The wicked shall be turned back [headlong into premature death], into Sheol (the place of the departed spirits of the wicked), even all the nations that forget or are forgetful of God."*

In the Living Bible, Psalms 9:17 (TLB) reads, *"The wicked shall be sent away to hell; this is the fate of all the nations forgetting the Lord."* Isn't this amazing to see the way translation has caused more harm than good in the Christian fold it seeks to represent? The very word hell, in the King James Version, is seen as Sheol in the Amplified bible, and hell in the Living Bible.

Let's see what other scriptures had to say in similar reference to the subject:

Job 14:13 (KJV): O that thou wouldest hide me in the grave, that thou wouldest keep me secret, until thy wrath be past, that thou wouldest appoint me a set time, and remember me!

(AMP): Oh, that You would hide me in Sheol (the unseen state), that You would conceal me until Your wrath is past, that You would set a definite time and then remember me earnestly [and imprint me on your heart]!

(TLB): "Oh that you would hide me with the dead and forget me there until your anger ends; but mark your calendar to think of me again!"

If the grave in this passage is therefore interpreted as Sheol, and we have seen the same Sheol translated as hell, why will God send Job, a righteous man, one that eschews evil, to hell only to be asked to remember him at the time appointed? Except that hell is not a place burning with fire as many have supposed, but rather, an abode of rest, the grave, not a burning pit of unquenchable hellfire.

With expressions like this, one will agree, it is quite disturbing to know, while seeking the truth, all you get is lies that have been told from one generation to another, to the point that many are confused more than they have ever thought they could be. The various versions have been the reason for this very confusion and discrepancies, for instance, in the book of Psalms, the Hebrew word Sheol, which also means hell, appeared eleven times or more. It is translated seven (7) times as hell, and four (4) times as grave. With this disparity, there is no course why the word hell could not be used to represent the same meaning seeing they all have same usage be it Sheol or hell. If this had been done, if they had written their work by the leading of the Holy Spirit, a lot would have been accomplished in the knowledge of the subject, regardless of the translator.

Let us see some scriptures used in the book of Psalms 6:5 (KJV): *"For in death there is no remembrance of thee: in the grave who shall give thee thanks?"* Psalms 6:5 (AMP): *"For in death there is no remembrance of You; in Sheol (the place of the dead) who will give You thanks?"*

Another scripture of interest will be when David spoke about the Lord, which in the New Testament Peter bared witness to in Psalms 16:10 and, Acts 2:27–32 (KJV). *"For thou wilt not leave my soul in hell; neither wilt thou suffer thine Holy One to see corruption."*

The Amplified Bible stated it saying,*"For You will not abandon me to Sheol (the place of the dead), neither will You suffer Your holy one [Holy One] to see corruption."*

And the Living Bible said, *"For you will not leave me among the dead; you will not allow your beloved one to rot in the grave."*

These various versions tell it all. What one of the translations speaks about Sheol, another calls it grave and the other, hell, but what they all have in common is that Sheol, hell, and grave, is the abode of the dead, a resting place from the turmoil of this life.

One beautiful thing about this particular passage is the fact that it applies to Christ and no other persons. Christ was clean and perfect in all his ways serving God, His will, and God's people. On his account, there was no record of him doing wrong or evil, yet the scripture presented him as one that goes down to the place of the wicked, according to popular belief of what hell is. Is it not that interesting? "*. . . Because thou wilt not leave my soul in hell, neither wilt thou suffer thine Holy One to see corruption. Thou hast made known to me the ways of life; thou shalt make me full of joy with thy countenance. Men and brethren, let me freely speak unto you of the patriarch David, that he is both dead and buried, and his sepulcher is with us unto this day. Therefore, being a prophet, and knowing that God had sworn with an oath to him, that of the fruit of his loins, according to the flesh, he would raise up Christ to sit on his throne; He seeing this before spake of the resurrection of Christ, that his soul was not left in hell, neither his flesh did see corruption. (This Jesus hath God raised up, whereof we all are witnesses*" (Acts 2:27–32).

If as holy as Jesus Christ is in all His glory, devotion, righteousness, and commitment to the things of God could go to hell, then, there is a need for a deeper and swift understanding. My question will be how can a savior be associated with hell, after paying the price for all sins and sinners, and be rewarded with the acclaimed burning hell? As an educated or inspired reader, if this understanding doesn't disturb you, then what will?

Be it as it may, I believe we all have an undisputable proof that hell or Sheol is not a burning furnace of fire nor is it a place of torment. Don't you agree? It will just be incomprehensible that anyone would think of Jesus of being in such a place after fulfilling his Father's will and dying. I am very sure that some or all of these translators must have had a dilemma assuming that Christ was in a burning hell theoretically.

Time will not permit us to examine all scriptures in reference to all these theses, but we will not do ourselves any good by not sharing some vital passages in relation to this understanding. *"Let me not be ashamed, O LORD; for I have called upon thee: let the wicked be ashamed and let them be silent in the grave. Let the lying lips be put to silence, which speak grievous things proudly and contemptuously against the righteous"* (Psalms 31:17–18 KJV).

In the Revised Standard Version (RSV), it reads, *"Let me not be put to shame, O LORD, for I call on thee; let the wicked be put to shame, let them go dumbfounded to Sheol. Let the lying lips be dumb, which speak insolently against the righteous in pride and contempt."*

In Psalms 49:14–15 (KJV), *"Like sheep they are laid in the grave; death shall feed on them; and the upright shall have dominion over them in the morning; and their beauty shall consume in the grave from their dwelling. But God will redeem my soul from the power of the grave: for he shall receive me. Selah."*

And in (RSV), *"Like sheep they are appointed for Sheol; Death shall be their shepherd; straight to the grave they descend, and their form shall waste away; Sheol shall be their home. But God will ransom my soul from the power of Sheol, for he will receive me. [Selah]"*

For detailed studies and for individuals who care to research the truth, I would advise that you get yourself the following Bibles: The King James Version, Amplified Bible, Revised Standard Version, and The Living Bible to mention a few, then get a word study Bible, by choosing the following scriptures as a possible place to start: Psalms 30:3, Psalms 88:3, Psalms 55:15, Psalms 89:48, Isaiah 53:10–12, Psalms 116:3, Psalms 141:7, Psalms 139:7–8, and Proverbs 1:12. For each scripture, use the various Bible versions to help navigate the truth about hell for your better understanding of the revelation of God on the subject. I promise you, you will appreciate the understanding of the knowledge of truth that you will receive.

Hell has its place, but man has denied its existence. If only they would pay close attention to vital details, then they would understand that the mystery of hell was clearly defined in the word of God. For instance, there is a scripture in the book of Isaiah that nailed hell to the existence of what we've all been discussing about the grave.

When an object is buried in the ground, or when an individual finds himself in a pit, he will clearly testify of the application of this scripture in Isaiah better, because then, he or she will understand the application of the grave, rather than the lies told us over centuries of failed gospel. The pit or the grave is usually warm at night and cold on a sunny day, so therefore, any who goes down to the belly of the pit or grave will come out cold in the course of the day. So are the dead; they remain cold constantly during the day and a burning heat at night according to Isaiah 47:14. *"Behold, they shall be as stubble; the fire shall burn them; they shall not deliver themselves from the power of the flame: there shall not be a coal to warm at, nor fire to sit before it."* Absolutely, there shall be no coal to warm, neither shall any deliver them from the burning of the heat. Isaiah was clearly showing us the state of the grave and not a burning hell. Another scripture in reference to the grave but used to typify hell is that which the Lord Jesus Christ mentioned in the book of Mark, where He said, *"Where their worm dieth not, and the fire is not quenched"* (Mark 9:44).

What the Lord is saying is very clear, if the fire burning is a literal flame in terms of hell, as the world claims it to be, why would the worms not die? Plainly establishing the proof that the fire spoken of is not a literal fire that is not quenched, neither is it a literal burning flame that scourges. But this is a good reasoning worms feed on dead bodies and indeed they never die. They are structured to live in the dust and they have the ability of weathering both the heat of the ground by night and the cold by day. Again, showing that the scripture of Isaiah 47:14

and Mark 9:44 are very similar in application. If hell therefore is to be considered as a place that is burning with fire and a house of torment to the wicked forever, that means to say the worms also, have gained eternity in the furnace of fire. This must be theoretically ridiculous. No one in their right mind should dare to assume that mare worms will coexist in judgment with wicked human souls who deserve the judgment they received. In my opinion, this would practically be unfair because the worms have not committed the sins men have indulged in. Again, worms are only there to feed on the human bodies that cannot inherit the kingdom of God. *"Now this I say, brethren, that flesh and blood cannot inherit the kingdom of God; neither doth corruption inherit incorruption"* (*1 Corinthians 15:50*). Just to straighten those who may want to wrest or exploit the scripture concerning the three Hebrew boys in the time of Babylon, who were thrown in the furnace of fire at the command of the kings, but were not burnt, they were not burnt because God never intended that any of his children be burnt with fire in the first place.

If we remember what Peter said of the Lord, that God will not leave the soul of Jesus Christ in hell neither will He suffer the Holy One to see corruption. He was inevitability expressing that the body of Jesus Christ never suffered any type of decay. There was no rottenness of His flesh because He is the Son of God, and He did perfect His time and work with God. Let us therefore draw understanding from these passages that hell is not a place of fury, torture, or torment, but a place of rest from the troubles of this life.

3

Where is Hell?

There are many who cannot really determine the true location of hell, because of the various myths surrounding it. It is very ironic that many can point to the sky and say, over there is heaven, and the earth, they clearly identify it's here, where we live. As for hell, only a few can point to its location or even know where to look. Many have sought to find the answer to this age-old mystery and are yet unable to pinpoint where it could be, because of lack of knowledge. Nevertheless, hell is where God intended it to be and has never moved or shifted. The answer is, hell is precisely beneath us, and anyone that seeketh it, seeketh it at the point of no return. It is to be left alone because it is not the place for the living, but a place for the dead. *"They shall go down to the bars of the pit, when our rest together is in the dust"(Job 17:16)*. If anyone remembers, pit, is one of the aforementioned names of hell that Bible translators used in describing Sheol, the abode of the dead.

Well, let us look at the scriptures to buttress the answer. As we just read in the book of Job, hell is below and beneath us, it is under the ground. As a matter of fact, the only thought that stands in similitude to judgment in reference to hell is the fact that destruction is an accomplice to the existence of hell. *"Hell and destruction are never full; so, the eyes of man are never satisfied" (Proverbs 27:20). The horseleach hath two daughters, crying, Give, give. There are three things that are never satisfied, yea, four things say not, it is enough: The grave; and the barren womb; the earth that is not filled with water; and the fire that saith not, It is enough"* (Proverbs 30:15–16). Whether a man is righteous or wicked, they all go down to the same place. Just as the thief on the cross went down to the grave or Sheol, so went Jesus to the same as we saw in the previous chapter of this book.

David prayed that God would let death seize upon his enemies, asking that they would go down quickly to their grave. *"Let death seize upon them and let them go down quick into hell: for wickedness is in their dwellings, and among them" (Psalms 55:15).*

David in all his knowledge knew that there is nowhere a man can hide from the reach of a determinate God. *"If I ascend up into heaven, thou art there: if I make my bed in hell, behold, thou are there" (Psalms 139:8).*

Solomon likewise was not silent in his understanding of hell, as he clearly spoke in the following passages, thereby establishing that hell is below our feet: *"Her feet go down to death; her steps take hold on hell" (Proverbs 5:5).*

"The way of life is above to the wise, that he may depart from hell beneath" (Proverbs 15:24). Even from the scriptures, the final destiny of the devil is ultimate destruction. *"Hell from beneath is moved for thee to meet thee at thy coming: it stirreth up the dead for thee, even all the chief ones of the earth; it hath raised up from their thrones all the kings of the nations"(Isaiah 14:9). "Yet thou shalt be brought down to hell, to the sides of the pit"(Isaiah 14:15).*

"Though they dig into hell, thence shall mine hand take them; though they climb up to heaven, thence will I bring them down" (Amos 9:2). This goes to explain the scripture that says, fear not he that can kill the body but cannot kill the soul. Rather fear He that is able to kill both

the body and the soul in hell. Meaning God, in his infinite power, can reach down to hell.

As we have read earlier and plainly so, hell is Sheol in the Hebrew word and Hades in the Greek, but commonly called grave in the English language by translation. So, apparently, hell is beneath the earth, and hell is where the dead remain until the time of their resurrection.

The grave, or hell, is inevitable for all who are dead whether they be righteous or unrighteous, whether they be elects or non-elects—the Bible shows us that in *Acts 2:29–32, "Men and brethren, let me freely speak unto you of the patriarch David, that he is both dead and buried, and his sepulcher is with us unto this day. Therefore, being a prophet, and knowing that God had sworn with an oath to him, that of the fruit of his loins, according to the flesh, he would raise up Christ to sit on this throne; He seeing this before spake of the resurrection of Christ, that his soul was not left in hell, neither his flesh did see corruption. This Jesus hath God raised up, whereof we all are witnesses."*

So, contrary to all religious believers, who believed that hell is a place burning with fire, Jesus our Lord, Savior, and Master went to the same place called hell, but thank God, His soul was not left there, neither did His body see corruption (decay). God the Father raised Him from hell, or rather from the abode of the dead mainly known as the grave, unto eternal glory to the witness of all who saw Him and all who chose to believe in Him.

Another point of reasoning will be where the Bible tells us that *"death and hell delivered up the dead, which were in them" (Revelation 20:13)*. Two important understandings to note in this passage is the use of the words "DEATH AND HELL" delivering up the dead, which were in THEM; showing us that the occupants of HELL and those that are DEAD must be brought out before the judgment seat of Christ. Why? Because hell is not the final place of judgment that awaits the ungodly and the unrighteous, neither can hell be forever, hence those that go down to it must resurrect. Another intriguing word used in this passage is, "them," showing us that their traditional belief of hell being a place of torment or judgment cannot be truth, being that the dead came out of them. *"And the sea gave up the dead which were in it; and death and hell delivered up the dead which were in them: and they were judged every man according to their works. And death and hell were cast into the lake of fire. This is the second death" (Revelation 20:13–14).* Meaning, the place of the dead is not few, nor is it single, as in terms of one location. As it reads again "DEATH AND HELL delivered up the DEAD which were in them." By the grace of God, I am sure we're getting an understanding that hell is the grave, and graves are many. So therefore, it is impossible for hell to be considered as one location.

Another school of thought is, if hell is a place where sinners are judged and transgressors are given their punishment, then there should be no need for the tenants or residents of hell to be brought up again for judgment according to their works to be judged the second time. This will be very unscriptural because that will mean double the judgment. This is an indication that someone or somebody has been spreading bad gospel across the globe that is not biblical. This is the theory of the religious world which is committed to the understanding that hell is a place of judgment. Saying, when a sinner dies without repentance or forgiveness, such an individual is considered to be in hell, or gone to hell. So, if God is going to bring those in hell out to face their judgment according to Revelation 20:13, what would we call it? Double jeopardy or failed system? There should be no need for individuals, supposedly condemned to hell, who should already be serving their sentences for the evil they committed, to be brought up again and be judged the second time. That will be quite ridiculous, don't you agree?

Any earthly court judge who does such will be considered in this life as incompetent of their position, not to mention God in his infinite knowledge, to make such mistake of double judgment in his commitment to truth and righteousness. This will be completely unrealistic. But thank God, our Father is an excellent judge, who knoweth the beginning and the end of all things, who also declares the end from the beginning. This error cannot be attributed to God because there is no truth in it.

Verse 14 of Revelation 20 gives us the comfort to know that the status of a sinner, is death. *"This is the second death" (Revelation 20:14).* A total state of oblivion, where the dead have no hope of return or resurrection. The Bible in warning us of rebellion, tells us that only the soul that sinneth shall die. *"Behold, all souls are mine; as the soul of the father, so also the soul of the son is mine: the soul that sinneth, it shall die" (Ezekiel 18:4).* Adam was not promised eternal life in rebellion, but was told by God, he is from the dust and to the dust shall he return. *"In the sweat of thy face shalt thou eat bread, till thou return unto the ground; for out of it wast thou taken: for dust thou art, and unto dust shalt thou return" (Genesis 3:19).*

Another area of understanding that might give every one of us clarity, might be the account of Jonah and his encounter with the whale on his way to Nineveh. Jonah 2:2 says, *"I cried by reason of mine affliction unto the LORD, and he heard me; out of the belly of hell cried I, and thou heardest my voice."*

Jonah may not be in the literal grave, but he described his temporal abode or habitation in the belly of a whale to be hell. There is no reason why Jonah would want to describe his existence in the whale's belly to be hell, other than the fact that he felt that he was in his state of oblivion, a state of no return, but thank God he got his deliverance. So shall the end be for all who serve the Lord faithfully shall rise out of the grave to answer to their reward.

If we look at the account of the transfiguration in Matthew 17:1–4, *"And after six days Jesus taketh Peter, James, and John his brother, and bringeth them up into a high mountain apart, and was transfigured before them: and his face did shine as the sun, and his raiment was white as the light. And behold, there appeared unto them Moses and Elias talking with him. Then answered Peter, and said unto Jesus, Lord, it is good for us to be here: if thou wilt, let us make here three tabernacles; one for thee, and one for Moses, and one for Elias."*

Jesus Christ took the disciples with Him to a high mountain according to the scripture, so that the disciples will witness the open appearance of Moses and Elijah. They did not descend from heaven, rather, they came out from beneath letting us know again that the dead are in the grave. While it is true that no one knows the burial place of either of these men, it is also obvious, they were not in heaven because Jesus himself said so in John 3:13, *"And no man hath ascended up to heaven, but he that came down from heaven, even the Son of man which is in heaven."* The location of hell should not be a controversy with any student of the Bible.

4

Wages and Gifts

It is imperative to understand the power of words, not because it is necessary to go back to some elementary school settings to seek the next intelligent teacher of language, but that through the use of words, we may come to an understanding of this subject matter. Wages is to work done, as gifts is to unmerited favor or a presented offering. Well, as the Lord demand of us saying, *"Come, let us reason together,"* perchance, this could be an open invitation to as many that might be seeking to know the truth concerning hell for themselves as well.

Regrettably true, the most familiar and often-quoted verse of the Bible seems to be most misunderstood by many in the platform of salvation, especially in relation to the subject of hell. John 3:16, which states, *"For God so loved the world, that He gave His only begotten Son, that whosoever believes in Him should not perish, but has everlasting life."* Could we assume millions routinely quote this verse of scripture, while ignoring an essential phrase within it?

Read it again! Those who receive salvation are promised that they "should not perish" but "have everlasting life"! If hell is a place of eternal torture and torment, then the residents of hell being tormented must also have eternal life, right? But wait a minute, the verse did not say "sinners should not perish," but rather, believers should be those that must not perish. How does the word "perish" relate to the popular teaching about hell and hellfire? Why did God inspire John to use the word perish if this is not what He meant? Jesus tells us in Revelation 14:10, *"The same shall drink of the wine of the wrath of God, which is poured out without mixture into the cup of his indignation; and he shall be tormented with fire and brimstone in the presence of the holy angels, and in the presence of the Lamb And the smoke of their torment ascendeth up for ever and ever: and they have no rest day nor night, who worship the beast and his image, and whosoever receiveth the mark of his name."*

According to the religious world, anyone who worships the beast and image *". . . shall drink of the wine of the wrath of God . . . and he shall be tormented with fire and brimstone . . . And the smoke of their torment ascendeth up forever and ever: and they have no rest day nor night."* Will this not be considered as hell? Just as many faith-based believers will assume this passage to describe that hell will literally burn continually through the ceaseless ages of eternity, without the proper understanding. However, I see the picture a little differently, and let me explain why. The Bible is very clear that the wicked will be destroyed. For example, *"The LORD preserveth all them that love him: but all the wicked will he destroy (Psalm 145:20).* Could "destroy" mean something different? A condition where the wicked will remain burning? No. This is in conflict with the context of the scriptures, because, "destroyed" means "not preserved, but perished," and as it is written, *"The wage of sin is death; but the gift of God is eternal life through Jesus Christ our Lord"* (Romans 6:23).

That's it, the wage of sin is death! Death cannot be spiritualized away in this passage. Death means ceasing to exist; perish, destroy, or cut off—not continuity.

When one is employed, he does receive regular paychecks. What he receives represents wages. Meaning, he must receive some form of compensation, an amount paid out to him for the work done. Proverbs

14:23 clearly states, *"In all labor there is profit . . . "* What about God? Does He ever pay wages for work? Yes, He does! Either for the work of righteousness or for evil. Notice in Revelation 22:12, *"And, behold, I come quickly; and my reward is with me, to give every man according as his work shall be."* Moreover, if it is God's will, then it is His bill. *"For God is not unrighteous to forget your work and labour of love, which ye have shewed toward his name, in that ye have ministered to the saints, and do minister"* (Hebrews 6:10).

The Bible clearly teaches that by divine decree there is an adequate just punishment for sin, and a commensurable gift from God for the right input of faith in all matters of righteousness. From the verse above, John 3:16, *"For God so loved the world, that He gave His only begotten Son, that whosoever believes in Him should not perish, but has everlasting life."* Eternal life is contrasted to DEATH, and to PERISHING! Therefore, the wage of sin is death, not eternal torture in hell as assumed by many who have interpreted the scripture to their own damnation.

There is no mystery regarding the meaning of wages that an employer pays an employee for his work. Therefore, there should be no confusion over the meaning of wages, when God says He will pay sinners for their evil works, meaning, He will pay the wicked a paycheck of death; can anyone imagine a reward of death? Death cannot be life in a place of torment. The Bible always means what it says, and says what it means, declaring plainly that it is its own best based commentary. It emphasizes that the scriptures cannot be broken. *"If he called them gods, unto whom the word of God came, and the scripture cannot be broken"* (John 10:35), and *"the word of God is truth"* (John 17:17). If we are to believe the Bible is unbreakable truth, then we must believe death means death, and life means life, nothing more or less! Some may want to spiritualize the meaning, saying there are spiritual and physical deaths, but whether we like it or not, the understanding of these straightforward verses should not be confused. Death, be it spiritualized, or carnalized, there is no alternative to death. The opposite of it is life and nothing less.

The best gift God the Father ever gave to humanity is still His Only Begotten Son, the Christ, whose name is the Lord Jesus as it is written, *"He that hath the Son hath life; and he that hath not the Son of God hath not life," (1 John 5:12).* God gave us His Son, not for us to escape eternal torment and smoky inferno of the acclaimed hell, but to be delivered from total annihilation from his presence. Our God created us to be daily His delight, to have the privilege of being in fellowship with Him day and night, rejoicing daily in His presence. *"And all things are of God, who hath reconciled us to himself by Jesus Christ, and hath given to us the ministry of reconciliation" (2 Corinthians 5:18–19).*

Therefore, to believe in the Lord Jesus is a gift. *"For unto you it is given in the behalf of Christ, not only to believe on him, but also to suffer for his sake" (Philippians 1:29).* In other words, whosoever believes in His Only Begotten Son, receives yet a greater gift of eternal life which is only resident in His Son. *"And this is the record that God hath given to us eternal life, and this life is in his Son. He that hath the Son hath life; and he that hath not the Son of God hath not life. These things have I written unto you that believe in the name of the Son of God; that ye may know that ye have eternal life, and that ye may believe in the name of the Son of God" (1 John 5:11–13).*

Adam and Eve rejoiced at the presence of God in the Garden of Eden, but when man fell, he inevitably invoked upon himself the punishment that carries with it the mandate of death sentence. The finality of sin is death. *"Behold, all souls are mine; as the soul of the father, so also the soul of the son is mine: the soul that sinneth, it shall die" (Ezekiel 18:4).*

God, unlike man, does not issue His paychecks on Fridays. Do you know God's paycheck to all who insist on doing evil and refuse the outstretched hand of salvation from His Only Begotten Son Jesus Christ is death? While this is a harsh saying, the immeasurable mercies of God the Father remain for all who choose to love Him, regardless of their trials or frailty. Alleluia.

A deep reality of the truth of wages and gifts is the fact that wages can be easily expended with the hope for more, but gifts are retained and cherished for as long as they can be kept. If we do not lose our salvation, then we do not need to bank on earning the wages of sin, which is nothing but death. Just like the wages could be used up, death will be the finality of sin. Sin is a product of time and will be finished on time. Sin will never follow man into eternity, just as it never came from hence. Only God has lived in eternity with His Son before there were any beginnings. Evidently, sin will not go into the ceaseless ages of eternity with God. Therefore, sin will be stopped at the time of the final judgment of God after the one thousand years reign of Christ is finished, which will be called, "the Millennium."

This will be the season when all whoremongers, liars, thieves, witches, idolaters, the wicked, and all evil spirits including the devil himself will be destroyed. God is going to pay them with death as a reward for all their wicked deeds, which they have ungodly committed. The will of God for all sinners who fail to repent before their passing from this life will be no life to repent with. They will be shut off from the presence of God forever. We may be wondering how, but read what He told Adam from the beginning: *"And unto Adam he said, Because thou hast hearkened unto the voice of thy wife, and hast eaten of the tree, of which I commanded thee, saying, Thou shalt not eat of it: cursed is the ground for thy sake; in sorrow shalt thou eat of it all the days of thy life; Thorns also and thistles shall it bring forth to thee; and thou shalt eat the herb of the field; In the sweat of thy face shalt thou eat bread, till thou return unto the ground; for out of it wast thou taken: for dust thou art, and unto dust shalt thou return" (Genesis 3:17–19).*

The promise of God to man for sinning against Him is that they will return to the dust. However, God has provided a substitute whom He has raised from the dust and set among princes. That substitute is Christ. The Bible says, *"God is of purer eyes than to behold evil, and canst not look on iniquity . . . " (Habakkuk 1:13).* God will glorify His begotten with the beauty of life from the dust of death, and raise Him unto glory. Men will see *"the exceeding greatness of his power to usward who believe, according to the working of his mighty power, which he wrought in Christ, when he raised him from the dead, and set him at his own right hand in the heavenly places (Ephesians 1:19–20).*

Nevertheless, God is merciful; He is righteous. He will not sit upon His throne watching men pop and fry, screaming and cursing all the remaining days of their miserable lives in hell, wishing for death. Should this be the case, the wicked will then be considered to be enjoying eternity with humankind, just like the believers. Then the scripture will be broken. What a tragedy this would be. Don't you think it is time to stop, reexamine the scripture, and reapproach the truth of God's word on hell, so that others may learn and understand? Let us reevaluate what we have known and have heard, instead of assuming we know and ignoring the truth, until the strike of doomsday.

5

Immortality of the Soul!

As we are deliberating on this interesting subject of hell, there is something we need to clarify next, and that is the immortality of the soul. Do people have immortal souls in relation to hell? As it seems, most people do not understand the relationship between the physical human body and the existence of the soul. In the Sunday schools of most fellowships, there is this understanding that humans are born with immortal souls. The common belief is that, upon death, the souls of the sinners go to hell forever, while those of true believers exit to take possessions in heaven, since they are considered immortals. Could this be true of the Bible? If sin's wages are death, could the Bible also teach that people have immortal souls? Can immortals die?

Before we proceed further, these are questions we need to unravel. It will be wise to know that the heavens are for God, who only hath immortality, therefore men cannot be immortal when they are still earthbound, until their change comes which will happen in a twinkle of an eye, according to the will of God based on the time appointed, not during or before the probation of man be completed. Please make an effort to get enlightened in the word of truth. Psalms 115:16 says, " *The heaven, even the heavens, are the LORD'S: but the earth hath he given to the children of men.* 1 Timothy 6:16 says, *(God) Who only hath immortality, dwelling in the light which no man can approach unto; whom no man hath seen, nor can see: to whom be honour and power everlasting. Amen."* See also in 1 Timothy 1:17, that shows that only *". . . God the King eternal, is immortal, invisible, the only wise God, to whom alone will be honour and glory forever and ever. Amen."*

To the ministers of the gospel who desire to be teachers of the law, this I say, you must first have an understanding of what to preach and of whom they affirm, not approach the scriptures out of head knowledge, but draw the strength of understanding that should spur their mind into the reasoning that the human souls are not immortals and can surely die. Because, men die daily, from the time of Adam until the last entity that just died. They died because they are not immortals but men. The question again is, can immortals die?

Traditionally, many believe heaven and hell are real to the point that everyone with an immortal soul must go somewhere when their physical life in this world ends. This belief is not unique to Christianity alone. Without controversy, a good majority of religions hold the same view that there is an aspect of the human person that lives on after this physical life has expired. This is a myth as we covered in the early chapters of this book. To tell you the truth, an immortal soul will defeat the physical or any form of death because immortality means indestructible. If a soul is eternal, then such a soul is unconquerable; death will never reign over such an entity.

MAN, SOUL, AND THE DUST

From the scriptures above, we must be clear that God alone is a patent immortal, not humans, regardless of any doctrinal source. Man was made from soil and dust, and by reason of God's breath, man became a living soul. *"And the LORD God formed man of the dust of the ground and breathed into his nostrils the breath of life, and man became a living soul"*

(Genesis 2:7). This verse does not say that men have souls inherently, but that Adam became a soul because he was made to have, or rather given, an active soul by the breath of the Almighty. The existence of the days of man was tied around his commitment to obedience. In other words, man was commissioned to keep his soul if he lived in the preference of obedience to his creator, God. As we all know, man failed his commission when the Lord God commanded man, saying, *"Of every tree of the garden thou mayest freely eat: But of the tree of the knowledge of good and evil, thou shalt not eat of it: for in the day that thou eatest thereof thou shalt surely die"* (Genesis 2:16–17). Though man was made a living soul, he was subject to death, contrary to the belief or understanding that humans are immortal.

Ezekiel, one of the major prophets of old, has this to say, *"The soul that sinneth, it shall die"* (Ezekiel 18:4). Death is the absence of life. A state of oblivion; it is not a transitional process. Death is not life in another place, but the absence of life or the state of being dead awaiting the moment of their resurrection.

Jesus, the Messiah of us all, further declares the frailty of the human soul in Matthew 10:28, *"And fear not them which kill the body, but are not able to kill the soul: but rather fear him which is able to destroy both soul and body in hell."* The Bible says that humans, and their earthly souls, can be DESTROYED! According to this verse, the soul can be exterminated as well as their bodies. We all recognize that the human body, the flesh, eventually dies and when it does, it naturally decomposes and becomes entirely "destroyed" due to the natural corruption of the environment in which they dwell. Therefore, the understanding that God can destroy all souls in hell should not be an amazement!

If an immortal quality exists in a human being, then it means that quality must depart from the body when it dies. That's a food for thought, isn't it? The typical understanding that the soul of a dead person moves out alive is a teaching that originates from some Greek culture and philosophies. The reason for saying that immortality must exit the human body, is that an immortal is known to be a never-dying body.

The New Bible Dictionary highlighted the nonbiblical nature of the soul's immortality: "The Greeks thought of the body as a hindrance to true life, and they tirelessly looked for when the soul of a man would be free from its corruptions." The understanding of life after death in terms of the immortality of the soul was the handwork of those who I might call the enemy of the truth.

According to their proclamation, the body goes to the grave at death, and the soul travels to a different place as a conscious entity. Such beliefs in an independent soul and body were also very popular in ancient Greece mythology and were taught widely by renowned men considered to be philosophers by those of old. These men, in their thinking, say, "the soul was a self-moving and inseparable part of the human structure"—showing that the soul does independently travel through the realms of porters and places.

While this remains a firm belief in the mind of many religious practitioners, it still stands as a fib. There is no validation of this claim in the sixty-six books of the Bible which we read and readily accept in the general Christendom.

THE SOUL AND THE CREATURE

The Hebrew word most often translated into English as "soul" in the Bible is *nephesh*. Strong's Talking Greek and Hebrew Dictionary of the Bible succinctly defines this word as meaning "a breathing creature." When used in the proper settings, it could be translated to man, also a creature with an active life.

In the Bible, nephesh does not mean a spirit entity or the spirit within a person. Rather, it usually means a physical, living, breathing creature. Occasionally, it could be interchanged in meaning such as breath, life, or person. Surprising to many, the term nephesh is used to refer not just to human beings, but also to animals. For example, *"God created great whales, and every living thing after its kind that moves beneath the water, and every winged fowl that flies in the air after their kind: and God saw that it was good" (Genesis 1:21).* The Hebrew word translated to "creature" in this verse, is nephesh. In the biblical account, these particular "souls," creatures of the sea, were made before the first human beings were formed and given life. This term is also applied to birds in verse 30, and land nephesh, including cattle and, "creeping" creatures, such as reptiles and insects in verse 24. Well, as it implies, if man is considered to be an immortal soul, then nephesh, likewise must also be considered as having an immortal soul, since the same Hebrew word used for man is considered to apply to nephesh alike. Yet no biblical scholars would seriously make such claims for nephesh. The truth is, the term soul refers to all living creatures, whether it's applicable to man or beast—not to some separate living essence temporarily inhabiting the body.

In the Old Testament, man is referred to as a "soul" (Hebrew nephesh) more than 130 times. The first place we find nephesh in reference to humankind is in Genesis 2:7: *"And the Lord God formed man of the dust of the ground and breathed into his nostrils the breath of life; and man became a living soul."* Other translations of the Bible state that man became a living "being," or "person." This verse does not say that Adam had an immortal soul, rather, it says that God breathed into Adam the "breath of life," and Adam became a living soul. At the end of his days, when the breath of life left Adam, he died and returned to dust.

Though some critics might want to pull a verse of scripture from the book of the preacher, saying that the spirit goes back to God, Ecclesiastes 12:7, let me remind us that the human life consists of three component factors, The spirit, soul, and body. 1 Thessalonians 5:23 says, *"And the very God of peace sanctify you wholly; and I pray God your whole spirit and soul and body be preserved blameless unto the coming of our Lord Jesus Christ."*

In various passages of the Bible such as Isaiah 26:9 that says, *"With my soul have I desired thee in the night; yea, with my spirit within me will I seek thee early: for when thy judgments are in the earth, the inhabitants of the world will learn righteousness."* The text clearly states that, with the soul man desires God but, with the spirit man seeketh, searches, and finds God. In other words, the soul has its functionality, completely different from the operation of the spirit. Let us consider another passage of scriptures in Isaiah 42:1, *"Behold my servant, whom I uphold; mine elect, in whom my soul delighteth; I have put my spirit upon him: he shall bring forth judgment to the Gentiles,"* and Matthew 12:18, *"Behold my servant, whom I have chosen; my beloved, in whom my soul is well pleased: I will put my spirit upon him, and he shall shew judgment to the Gentiles."*

You see, God delighted in Christ with his soul, but He placed forth His spirit in Him. God did not place His soul in the Son, His elect, what He gave to His Son was His spirit. Showing us that the soul in all beings is not malignant, nor does it move about without the body.

The Old Testament plainly teaches that the soul that is placed in man, or beast, dies. God told Adam and Eve, two "living souls," that they would "surely die" if they disobeyed Him in Genesis 2:17, *"But of the tree of the knowledge of good and evil, thou shalt not eat of it: for in the day that thou eatest thereof thou shalt surely die."* God also told Adam that He had taken him from the dust of the earth, and He would return him to the dust. *"In the sweat of thy face shalt thou eat bread, till thou return unto the ground; for out of it wast thou taken: for dust thou art, and unto dust shalt thou return" (Genesis 3:19)*. Clearly showing that man became something different from the dust that was made of because of the impartation of the breath of the Almighty.

Among the most emphasized statements in the Bible about what happens to the soul at death, that of Ezekiel 18:4 and 18:20 stand out completely. Both passages clearly state that "the soul who sins shall die." Again, the word for "soul" in reference here is nephesh.

In fact, this same word was even used for corpses (dead bodies) according to the King James Version with strong numbers.

"What man soever of the seed of Aaron is a leper, or hath a running issue; he shall not eat of the holy things, until he be clean. And whoso toucheth anything that is unclean by the dead, or a man whose seed goeth from him" (Leviticus 22:4).

"Command the children of Israel, that they put out of the camp every leper, and every one that hath an issue, and whosoever is defiled by the dead" (Numbers 5:2).

"And the priest shall offer the one for a sin offering, and the other for a burnt offering, and make an atonement for him, for that he sinned by the dead, and shall hallow his head that same day"(Numbers 6:11).

"And there were certain men, who were defiled by the dead body of a man, that they could not keep the Passover on that day: and they came before Moses and before Aaron on that day: And those men said unto him, We are defiled by the dead body of a man: wherefore are we kept back, that we may not offer an offering of the LORD in his appointed season among the children of Israel? And Moses said unto them, stand still, and I will hear what the LORD will command concerning you. And the LORD spake unto Moses, saying, speak unto the children of Israel, saying, if any man of you or of your posterity shall be unclean by reason of a dead body, or be in a journey afar off, yet he shall keep the Passover unto the LORD" (Numbers 9:6–10).

Not only do all these scriptures show that the soul indeed can, and does die, but the soul is identified as a physical being—not a separate spiritual entity with existence independent of its physical host. The scriptures tell us that the dead have no consciousness: "For the living know that they will die; but the dead know nothing." *For the living know that they shall die: but the dead know not anything, neither have they any more a reward; for the memory of them is forgotten."* Meaning, the dead are not conscious in some other state or place, but are concluded dead in terms of movement, being motionless, lifeless, and inactive. Their memory, their knowledge, their hatred, and ability to love, are completely dysfunctional. They have no more a reward or part of anything that is being done under the heavens. *"Whatsoever thy hand findeth to do, do it with thy might; for there is no work, nor device, nor knowledge, nor wisdom, in the grave, whither thou goest" (Ecclesiastes 9:10).*

Although so many believers have induced themselves to believe they no more need the Old Testament for their belief and references, declaring, they are no more under the law. Well, while that may be true to some extent, the teachings and understanding of hell are just as applicable to the Old as well as the New Testament.

Likewise, the New Testament contains several statements confirming that the wicked who refuse to repent will die—permanently. In Matthew 7:13–14, *"Enter ye in at the strait gate: for wide is the gate, and broad is the way, that leadeth to destruction, and many there be which go in there at: Because strait is the gate, and narrow is the way, which leadeth unto life, and few there be that find it."* In exhorting His disciples to choose the way that leads to life, Jesus stated that the end of those who do not choose life has bought for themselves destruction. He contrasts the pathway of destruction with the way of righteousness, telling us, *"Narrow is the gate and difficult is the way which leads to life, and there are few who finds it,"* meaning if a man finds the way of life, such a man has purchased unto himself the benefit of keeping his soul from total annihilation. Jesus, however, made it quite clear that utter destruction includes both "soul and body" thereby making it impossible for the soul to live on after the body has suffered destruction. *"And fear not them which kill the body but are not able to kill the soul: but rather fear him which is able to destroy both soul and body in hell" (Matthew 10:28).*

The Greek word for soul, "suche," refers to the physical conscious existence. Some Bible verses teach that we have an immortal soul, but the Apostle Paul stated that the wicked will die. In Romans 6:20–23, he talks about those who were slaves of sin and speaks of them saying, *"The end of such is death."*

Therefore, those who are slaves of sin, who habitually commit sin, and stay in sin, can have it settled in their mind that they could perish completely in sin someday, if they fail to repent before the day of their death. If such one refuses, then they shall have eternity to regret, because they would have succeeded in voiding out their lives from the resurrection. For many who would have attempted to redefine death in their own understanding and usage of scriptural passages to mean merely separation from God or a state of one asleep, Romans 6:23 declares plainly, *"For the wages of sin is death, but the gift of God is eternal life in Christ Jesus our Lord."* Note, however, that death here is directly contrasted with eternal life, meaning, the reward for sinning is death, not eternal life somewhere with misery.

How then, can death involve eternal existence through an immortal soul? This verse establishes two crucial truths for all to see. First, the punishment of the wicked is death, utter cessation of life, not a life of eternal suffering in another place. For the benefit of clearer understanding, read Ecclesiastes 9:5–6,10: *"For the living know that they shall die: but the dead know not anything, neither have they any more a reward; for the memory of them is forgotten. Also, their love, and their hatred, and their envy, is now perished; neither have they any more a portion forever in anything that is done under the sun."* *"Whatsoever thy hand findeth to do, do it with thy might; for there is no work, nor device, nor knowledge, nor wisdom, in the grave, whither thou goest."* And John 3:16: *"For God so loved the world, that he gave His only begotten Son, that whosoever believeth in him should not perish, but have everlasting life."*

Secondly, no one has eternal life through a supposed immortal soul. Eternal life is something God must give unto us through our Savior at the resurrection of the first fruits unto God and His Son Jesus Christ (the bride), Jesus the Messiah. In 1 Timothy 6:16, Paul also tells us that God alone *"has immortality, dwelling in the light which no man can approach unto; whom no man hath seen, nor can see: to whom be honour and power everlasting. Amen."*

Paul makes a similar statement in Galatians 6:8, *"The one who sows to please his sinful nature, from that nature will reap destruction; the one who sows to please the Spirit, from the Spirit will reap eternal life."* Would this not show what happens to unrepentant sinners? The answer eventually is, they will reap destruction, wasting and perishing away, but those who repent and obey God will ultimately receive eternal life.

Just like James said in his writings, " . . . *friendship with the world is enmity against God" (James 4:4–5)*. Friendship with the world is such that has no place for God in their soul and spiritual walk with God.

The Bible told us that God will not leave the soul of the righteous in hell. Jesus Christ's soul was not left in hell according to Acts 2:30–32. The soul of the righteous must await the resurrection of our Lord and Savior Jesus Christ. If Jesus resurrected from the grave, we also must resurrect from the grave at some point in our state of oblivion. The soul of the righteous man as well as that of the wicked must resurrect, because their souls are mortal. The soul does not die until the final judgment at the end of age. Just as what has been said, the soul does not move out alive nor journey anywhere.

Only after the reward of righteousness or the condemnation of the unjust takes place, only then will the final fate of the soul of man be determined that such soul is mortal, or be destroyed. The soul of man could last a lifetime and beyond. The soul is what will couple up with the heavenly body that is to be given at the resurrection. *"For we know that if our earthly house of this tabernacle were dissolved, we have a building of God, a house not made with hands, eternal in the heavens. For in this we groan, earnestly desiring to be clothed upon with our house which is from heaven: If so, be that being clothed we shall not be found naked. For we that are in this tabernacle do groan, being burdened: not for that we would be unclothed, but clothed upon, that mortality might be swallowed up of life"(2 Corinthians 5:1–4)*.

This is why Jesus, at the event of the death of Lazarus, referred to the state of the dead as one that sleepeth. The soul will remain silent in the grave, or wherever life exited itself from such soul. We all will remember that the breath of the Almighty was instrumental to man becoming a living soul, as written in Genesis 2. In other words, the existence of man was only a base clay with the soul lifeless in it. Not until the Almighty breathed upon its nostrils, did man become a living soul, showing that without the breath of the Almighty, man will remain a lifeless entity.

The flesh and blood of man will inherit corruption and decay, because it cannot inherit the kingdom of God if God did not quicken it with his breath. For corruption must be swallowed up by incorruption. And in a twinkle of an eye, we shall be changed. *"Behold, I shew you a mystery; We shall not all sleep, but we shall all be changed, in a moment, in the twinkling of an eye, at the last trump: for the trumpet shall sound, and the dead shall be raised incorruptible, and we shall be changed"* (1 Corinthians 15:51–52).

Like Paul expressed, we shall not all sleep, but be changed. If the body of man, made like unto flesh and blood will perish, then it is obvious that when we shall awake out of the so-said sleep, we will wake up to inherit, and inhabit a new body prepared in heaven, *"a body not made with hands, eternal in heaven"*(2 Corinthians 5:1).

The mortal souls of men will put on or couple up, with the body God shall give to every man according to their works and positioning in God. These are the bodies immortal, celestial, and terrestrial, and if we serve obediently, submissively, and devotionally, they shall be ours.

"All flesh is not the same flesh: but there is one kind of flesh of men, another flesh of beasts, another of fishes, and another of birds. There are also celestial bodies, and bodies terrestrial: but the glory of the celestial is one, and the glory of the terrestrial is another" (1 Corinthians 15:39–40).

"To them who by patient continuance in well doing seek for glory and honour and immortality, eternal life"(Romans 2:7).

NO IMMORTALITY WITHOUT A RESURRECTION

On this account, can anyone say the soul of man is an immortal soul? Or does he have an immortal body? No! The Bible declares plainly that the place of man in creation is temporal, and of the dust of the earth. There are no immortal qualities about dust at all. We receive this life of immortality from God, through a resurrection that is soon to come at the close of the church age, which means being brought back to life in a body, raised from the dead as Jesus was. The Bible clearly states that man eventually must put on immortality at the resurrection. If they are chosen vessels, not at the end of his physical life, but at the end. *"Now this I say, brethren, that flesh and blood cannot inherit the kingdom of God; neither doth corruption inherit incorruption. Behold, I shew you a mystery; We shall not all sleep, but we shall all be changed, in a moment, in the twinkling of an eye, at the last trump: for the trumpet shall sound, and the dead shall be raised incorruptible, and we shall be changed. For this corruptible must put on incorruption, and this mortal must put on immortality. So, when this corruptible shall have put on incorruption, and this mortal shall have put on immortality, then shall be brought to pass the saying that is written, Death is swallowed up in victory"* (1 Corinthians 15:50–54). This physical life needs a giveaway for the glorious life of eternity to become manifested.

Until that time, man has no more pre-eminence than nephesh, nor does man have some spiritual soul with conscious awareness independent of the physical body. *"I said in mine heart concerning the estate of the sons of men, that God might manifest them, and that they might see that they themselves are beasts. For that which befalleth the sons of men befalleth beasts; even one thing befalleth them: as the one dieth, so dieth the other; yea, they have all one breath; so that a man hath no preeminence above a beast: for all is vanity. All go unto one place; all are of the dust, and all turn to dust again. Who knoweth the spirit of man that goeth upward, and the spirit of the beast that goeth downward to the earth?"* (Ecclesiastes

3:18–21). This has been proven time and time again, when individuals have gone into comas for weeks, months, and sometimes even years at a time, then emerge from that comatose state with little or no memory or a recollection of the passage of time at all. Now let's reason beyond this, if one had a soul that existed independently of the human body, wouldn't that soul have some memory or consciousness of what they are doing during the months or years the body was in the state of coma? If that ever happens wouldn't that be a powerful and logical proof of the existence of an independent soul within the human body? But no one has ever reported any such happenings, in spite of thousands of such occurrences. This fact, likewise, supports what the Bible teaches, that consciousness ceases at death. Only through a resurrection to life will consciousness return, because man will no longer be limited in their power to see through the ages of time, but will now be able to relate with what the future holds due to the spiritual and supernatural nature that they will possess.

Though some believe that there are various scriptures supporting the belief in an immortal soul, let's consider some of these passages and understand what they really say.

Matthew 10:28 on destroying soul and body in hell: *"And do not fear those who kill the body but cannot kill the soul. But rather fear Him who is able to destroy both soul and body in hell."*

Was Jesus advocating in this verse that the soul lives on after death as an immortal? Not at all. On the contrary, if you look at this scripture closely, you see that Jesus is actually saying that the soul can be destroyed. Jesus, in warning men of his day about the judgment of God, He said, you need not fear those who can destroy only the physical human body (*soma* in the Greek) but fear Him (God) who is also able to destroy both the body and soul, in hell. This scripture further shows that no one person can destroy the soul of any human, yet the soul is capable of being destroyed by Him, the soul maker. *"Behold, all souls are* mine; as the soul of the father, so also the soul of the son is mine: the soul that sinneth, it shall die" (Ezekiel 18:4).

God can raise anyone to conscious life again either soon after death, or after the resurrection; see Matthew 9:23–25 where Jesus Christ raised the ruler's daughter. In chapter 27:52 of the book of Matthew, many righteous dead were raised by God to prove there will be a resurrection for His Son. In John 11:43–44, Lazarus was raised from the dead; Acts 9:40–41, Dorcas was restored back to life; 20:9–11, Eutycus received life from the dead by the hand of Paul the Apostle; or in the days to come, after Christ returns to the earth, in Revelation 20:4–6, many righteous dead will resurrect to rule and reign with Christ through the millennium. Those who died are not ultimately gone forever because there is still the option for resurrection, both to the good and evil.

We must have a proper fear of God, who alone can remove one's physical life, and all its bearings until the possibility of any later resurrection to life. When God destroys the body and the soul in "hell," that person's destruction is permanent; Revelation 20:13–15 (*we will deal with this scripture in more detail later in this study*).

What is the "hell" spoken of in this verse? The Greek word used here is Gehenna, which comes from the combination of two Hebrew words, *Gai* and *Hinnom*, meaning "Valley of Hinnom." The term originally referred to a valley on the south side of Jerusalem in which pagan deities were worshipped. Again, because of its reputation as an abominable place; *"And they built the high places of Baal, which are in the valley of the son of Hinnom, to cause their sons and their daughters to pass through the fire unto Molech; which I commanded them not, neither came it into my mind, that they should do this abomination, to cause Judah to sin"(Jeremiah 32:35).*

This land later became a garbage dump where trash was burned making the word "Gehenna" to be synonymous with "a place of burning"—a site used to dispose of useless things. Only God can utterly destroy human existence and eliminate any hope of a resurrection. The scriptures teach that God will, in the future, burn up the incorrigibly wicked in an all-consuming fire, turning them to ashes, annihilating them forever; *"And ye shall tread down the wicked; for they shall be ashes under the soles of your feet in the day that I shall do this, saith the LORD of hosts"* (Malachi 4:3).

Many may be confused by the expression the Apostle Paul uses in one of his letters to the Thessalonians saying, *"Now may the God of peace Himself sanctify you completely; and may your whole spirit, soul, and body be preserved blameless at the coming of our Lord Jesus Christ"* in 1 Thessalonians 5:23. So What exactly does Paul mean by the phrase "spirit, soul, and body"? Let us see.

By "spirit," Paul means the nonmaterial component that is joined to the physical human brain to form the human mind. This spirit is not conscious of itself, rather, it gives the brain the ability to reason, create, and analyze our existence; see also Job 32:8, *"But there is a spirit in man: and the inspiration of the Almighty giveth them understanding."* In 1 Corinthians 2:11, *"For what man knoweth the things of a man, save the spirit of man which is in him? even so the things of God knoweth no man, but the Spirit of God."* The Spirit is what the Lord has given to man to help him stay in touch with his destiny, and his eternity. By this God-given Spirit, man is able to search internally for their strength, weakness, faults, and the pathway by which he grows or goes thereby. The Bible says to us that, *"the Spirit of man is the candlestick of God"* (Proverbs 20:27). You can be surer today of our salvation than before because of the genuine sanctity of our heart in bringing us to accountability and to the acknowledgment of the truth because of the candle of the Lord burning within us. In Proverbs 20:27, *"The spirit of man is the candle of the LORD, searching all the inward parts of the belly."*

By "soul," the person's physical being, with its consciousness, consisting of his intellect, sensibility, and his will, is able to live above death, or any form of impending judgment. The soul is an element that the spirit inhabits. This is why we need our soul to be sanctified, so that we can escape the eternal abode in hell. The sanctification of our soul causes us to not be dead to our existence, so that we fail not in fulfilling the purpose of God concerning us.

By "body," Paul means a physical body of flesh. In short, Paul wished for the whole person, including the mind, the vitality of conscious life, and the physical body, to be sanctified and blameless. The body is the vehicle that was built and was trusted to carry the spirit and the soul, to accomplish whatever tasks the Lord assigns. If the spirit of a man be right, then his soul stands guiltless of hell, and that makes us more profitable for the Kingdom of our God.

Another critical point to note, or line of thought to consider, will be the event of the souls that will cry out.

SOULS OF THE SLAIN CRYING OUT?

Revelation 6:9–10:

"When He opened the fifth seal or the apocalypse, the Bible says the soul that hath been slain will cry out from under the alter as John said, I saw under the altar the souls of those who had been slain for the word of God and for the testimony which they held. And they cried with a loud voice, saying, 'How long, O Lord, holy and true, until You judge and avenge our blood on those who dwell on the earth?'"

To understand this scripture, we must remember its context. John was witnessing a vision while he was "in the Spirit" in Revelation 4:2, *"And immediately I was in the spirit: and behold, a throne was set in heaven, and one sat on the throne."* Under inspiration, he was seeing futuristic events depicted in symbolism. The fifth seal is figurative of the Tribulation to come, a time of world turmoil preceding the Lord's return. In this vision, John saw under the altar the souls of the martyred believers who sacrificed their lives for their faith in God. These souls figuratively cried out, *"Avenge our blood!"* This can be compared to Abel's blood metaphorically crying out to God from the ground in Genesis 4:10, *"And he said, what hast thou done? The voice of thy brother's blood crieth unto me from the ground."* Though, neither sleeping souls, nor blood of the dead, can actually speak out, for Ecclesiastes 9:5–6,10 says, *"For the living know that they shall die: but the dead know not anything, neither have they any more a reward; for the memory of them is forgotten. Also, their love, and their hatred, and their envy, is now perished; neither have they any more a portion forever in anything that is done under the sun. Whatsoever thy hand findeth to do, do it with thy might; for there is no work, nor device, nor knowledge, nor wisdom, in the grave, whither thou goest."* These phrases intently demonstrate that God, being a righteous judge of justice will not forget the evil deeds of humankind perpetrated against His righteous followers.

These souls will cry out for vengeance from their resting places of the grave, or Sheol as called in the Hebrew tongue. Just as Lazarus could hear him from his dead state of four days, so, Abel's blood cried out, but how can the blood of a dead man cry out except there is something that is within the man that could speak, something within him that could reach out to God beyond the flesh, beyond the earth, and beyond religiosity, which in my opinion, could be his soul. So, to come to reality or reasoning, if the soul of Abel, Samuel, Elisha, or Lazarus could react or speak, then it is obvious that their soul remained where they are buried and did not move out alive, flying around somewhere still tussling, or reacting in some leisure limbo outside of the eyes of human reach.

As Jesus said, which we mentioned earlier, the soul of the mortals is at rest when they pass on, or are considered sleeping, not dead. Even as we would see in the encounter of Saul the King of Israel, with the witch in Endor. *"Then said Saul unto his servants, seek me a woman that hath a familiar spirit, that I may go to her, and enquire of her. And his servants said to him, Behold, there is a woman that hath a familiar spirit at Endor. And Saul disguised himself, and put on other raiment, and he went, and two men with him, and they came to the woman by night: and he said, I pray thee, divine unto me by the familiar spirit, and bring me him up, whom I shall name unto thee. And the woman said unto him, Behold, thou knowest what Saul hath done, how he hath cut off those that have familiar spirits, and the wizards, out of the land: wherefore then layest thou a snare for my life, to cause me to die? And Saul sware to her by the LORD, saying, As the LORD liveth, there shall no punishment happen to thee for this thing. Then said the woman, whom shall I bring up unto thee? And he said, Bring me up Samuel. And when the woman saw Samuel, she cried with a loud voice: and the woman spake to Saul, saying, Why hast thou deceived me? for thou art Saul. And the king said unto her, Be not afraid: for what sawest thou? And the woman said unto Saul, I saw gods ascending out of the earth. And he said unto her, what form is he of? And she said, an old man cometh up; and he is covered with a mantle. And Saul perceived that it was Samuel, and he stooped with his face to the ground, and bowed himself. And Samuel said to Saul, why hast thou disquieted me, to bring me up? And Saul answered, I am sore distressed; for the Philistines make war against me, and God is departed from me, and answereth me no more, neither by prophets, nor by dreams: therefore, I have called thee, that thou mayest make known unto me I shall do"* (1 Samuel 28:7–15).

At the raising up of Samuel in verse 15, Samuel said to Saul, why has thou disquieted me, to bring me up. Take note, not to bring me down from the sky, or from heaven, or limbo. He said why has thou (disquieted) disturbed me, meaning, his soul was present with him, he was resting, sleeping, or, in truth, waiting for his appointed time like Job. *"So man lieth down, and riseth not: till the heavens be no more, they shall not awake, nor be raised out of their sleep. O that thou wouldest hide me in the grave, that thou wouldest keep me secret, until thy wrath be past, that thou wouldest appoint me a set time, and remember me! If a man die, shall he live again? All the days of my appointed time will I wait, till my change come. Thou shalt call, and I will answer thee: thou wilt have a desire to the work of thine hands" (Job 14:12–15).* Samuel felt disturbed and disquieted because he was waiting for his appointed time when God, his Father, will wake him up. He was waiting for his change to come. He was waiting for the voice of his bridegroom to come calling. The second fact to review is that Samuel was brought up from the grave, not brought down. If Saul was in limbo, then, he would have been brought down from the man-made, self-acclaimed, state of limbo. Certainly, these verses do not describe living souls migrating to heaven.

The Bible confirms that *"no one has ascended to heaven but He who came down from heaven, that is, the Son of Man who is in heaven [Jesus Christ]" (John 3:13).* Even the righteous King David, a man after God's own heart *(Acts 13:22),* was described by Peter as being *"dead and buried" (Acts 2:29),* not alive in heaven or some other state or location *(verse 34).* So, let's read these passages: John 3:13, *"And no man hath ascended up to heaven, but he that came down from heaven, even the Son of man which is in heaven."* Acts 13:22, *"And when he had removed him, he raised up unto them David to be their king; to whom also he gave testimony, and said, I have found David the son of Jesse, a man after mine own heart, which shall fulfill all my will."* Acts 2:29, *"Men and brethren, let me freely speak unto you of the patriarch David, that he is both dead and buried, and his sepulchre is with us unto this day."*

6

Lazarus and the Rich Man

The parable of Lazarus and the rich man is one of the most used theses to explain the riddles of hell. Many have invented their own side of the story, making it sound so real. I call it a riddle, because it is a parable that must be understood and evidently be interpreted as such.

It is important that we do not make assumptions about the scriptures or imply our own private interpretations. All scriptures, the Bible says, *"are by the inspiration of God"* (*2 Timothy 3:16*). Moreover, because of the inspiration of the Almighty, the need for understanding of such scriptures becomes a necessity. *"By the Spirit, He gave man the opportunity to profit withal"* (*1 Corinthians 12:7*). *"Surely, thou hast spoken in mine hearing, and I have heard the voice of thy words, saying"* (*Job 33:8*).

Having read so far on this expository topic of hell, I am sure your next question will be, what actually is the parable of the "Rich Man and Lazarus?" Or "What has it got to do with hell?"

For this parable is what is expressively used to explain the state of hell, especially after knowing that the souls of mortal men and women, young or old, White, Black, or Hispanic, do not move out alive, neither exist in an obscure location distanced from their loved ones.

Now, it becomes necessary for us to look at this controversial area of the word of God, especially as it references one of the most popular stories or parables of Jesus Christ, which many, for lack of proper understanding over the centuries gone by, may have misrepresented. Some, for fear of theological defiance, have concurred with others to claim this parable to be literal, not willing to accept it as a parable but as a literal event that did transpire, which absolutely is not true. Very many individuals somehow do believe significantly according to the parable, that the rich man is in hell, while the poor man, being a beggar, is comfortably seated in heaven on Abraham's bosom. Though the scripture made no such assertion of the definite location as to the beggar being in heaven, or Abraham seated in the heavens. We find this narrative in Luke 16:19–31.

The urgency in digesting this area of understanding in the lesson of hell, is of utmost importance. The reason being, that this is one of the statutory passages of thought in the scriptures that suggest torment or torture in hell, Sheol, or Hades. The Bible tells us plainly, *"for there is no work, nor device, nor knowledge, nor wisdom, in the grave, whither thou goest"* (*Ecclesiastes 9:10*).

One point to note is the fact that the Bible did not specify anything about the virtue of either of these men, the rich man or Lazarus, and neither was anything in the narrative that depicted their spiritual lifestyle. Whether they were sinful or righteous, it was not clearly stated. The commonality between both of these men in this script, was that they both died, and the poor man was carried to Abraham's bosom by an angel, and the other being a rich man, was in hell, dying of thirst and anguish, and in torment cried out for a drop of water.

Well, if the scriptures remain unbroken, then it will be clear that Abraham's bosom would have rotted a long while ago, because Abraham is long dead and buried according to Genesis 25:10. *"The field which Abraham purchased of the sons of Heth: there was Abraham buried, and Sarah his wife."*

Furthermore, if the status of a person being rich or poor determined their placement in the kingdom, then men like David, Solomon, Abraham, Barnabas, and many more, the likes of whom we may have known or read about, are most likely to end up miserable, and the scripture in Deuteronomy 8:18 would have been their pitfall. As it is written, *"But thou shalt remember the LORD thy God: for it is he that giveth thee power to get wealth."* In other words, those who have been made rich among the fellowship will have eternity to regret. Why? Because the status of the rich according to the parable, is to end up in hell, as many have believed over the decades. This will be entirely absurd as it is the Lord that gave the power to make such wealth. So, He giving one the right to have wealth and then turn such one into hell material will be most ridiculous. I am sure you will agree.

The probable question does stand out: Should we contemplate poverty as a status for us to make it to the kingdom of our God, or for us to be accepted in the will of God? The answer will remain No!

The economic status of a person does not interfere with their placement in the inheritance.

With this being said, forthwith we must agree, there is a missing link in the understanding of this parable, and before we can fully digest the content of this text, we must realize that Jesus was speaking to the Pharisees and the bystanders of his day in figurative speeches which did not start in the sixteenth chapter, but spanned from the fifteenth chapter of the book of Luke where he started out with the parable of *"The Lost Sheep," "The Lost Coin," "The Prodigal Son," "The Dishonest Steward,"* and finally the parable of *"Lazarus and the Rich Man."* While we have all these parables unplanned but yet stated, we will only concern ourselves with the subject matter, and through the help of the Holy Spirit, we should be ready to resolve the mystery involved in this parable with good understanding through the wisdom of God and to know the truth and the light behind it. With all that being said, let us therefore familiarize ourselves with how Jesus laid out this said parable from the book of Luke 16:19–31.

"There was a certain rich man, which was clothed in purple and fine linen, and fared sumptuously every day: And there was a certain beggar named Lazarus, which was laid at his gate, full of sores, And desiring to be fed with the crumbs which fell from the rich man's table: moreover the dogs came and licked his sores. And it came to pass, that the beggar died, and was carried by the angels into Abraham's bosom: the rich man also died and was buried; And in hell he lift up his eyes, being in torments, and seeth Abraham afar off, and Lazarus in his bosom. And he cried and said, Father Abraham, have mercy on me, and send Lazarus, that he may dip the tip of his finger in water, and cool my tongue; for I am tormented in this flame. But Abraham said, Son, remember that thou in thy lifetime receivedst thy good things, and likewise Lazarus evil things: but now he is comforted, and thou art tormented. And beside all this, between us and you there is a great gulf fixed: so that they which would pass from hence to you cannot; neither can they pass to us, that would come from thence. Then he said, I pray thee therefore, father, that thou wouldest send him to my father's house: For I have five brethren; that he may testify unto them, lest they also come into this place of torment. Abraham saith unto him, they have Moses and the prophets; let them hear them. And he said, Nay, Father Abraham: but if one went unto them from the dead, they will repent. And he said unto him, if they hear not Moses and the prophets, neither will they be persuaded, though one rose from the dead."

WHY IN PARABLE?

Having read and understood what Jesus Christ spoke was in parable, we need to find out why Jesus spoke to these men and women of his day in symbolic language or may I say in parabolic sense. In looking at Matthew 13:34, *"All these things spake Jesus unto the multitude in parables; and without a parable spake he not unto them."* It was clear that

Jesus did not quite communicate to the general masses of his day in plain language except in parables. We will notice that in verse 10 of the same passage, the disciple went on ahead to ask the Lord why he had to speak in parable among many listeners and not in direct speeches to the people. Before we hear what Christ responded to them, it would be wise to establish the fact that all in God's house are usually not on the same level of growth, assimilation, or even callings. While some lessons or messages are reflective on some, at the same time, they could, in the same manner, be deflective on others and only those whom it is meant for will fully grasp the intent of such messages, prophecies, or instructions with the understandings that pertain to their lives.

In Matthew 13:11, *"He answered and said unto them, because it is given unto you to know the mysteries of the kingdom of heaven, but to them it is not given."* It is a blessing, among many who hear the word, that you could find your place for comfort; you could gain an understanding, because to you it is given. To you the excellency of knowledge is given. And to you the knowledge of the world to come is given. This I say is a privilege.

The answer of the Lord clearly shows He wanted the apostles to understand these sayings of His, or rather, that they will understand how God the Father has given them the ability to comprehend the mysteries of what He has to say to empower them into leadership positions, while the others are meant to be just followers.

I pray that in your dealings with this subject, God will fortify you into a revelatory position above your equals in the knowledge of His will by Christ Jesus. This is because you are a proper child by your Father; proper children will always hear their Father and a stranger they will not follow. Those who aren't proper children, probably do not hear, until they end up in conditions they cannot get out of, or in some form of spiritual captivity. The Bible says the *"wise man heareth and get wiser and the foolish rejects instruction and they are destroyed"* (Proverbs 9:9).

If we look into verse 13–17 of Matthew 13, we will see why Jesus spoke to these other men in parables: though they have eyes, they cannot see and ears, they cannot hear neither could they perceive with their hearts. They've had the laws and the prophets but refuse to identify the voice of God for their day even as Apostle Paul puts it: " . . . *It was necessary that the word of God should first have been spoken to you: but seeing ye put it from you, and judge yourselves unworthy of everlasting life, lo, we turn to the Gentiles" (Acts 13:46).*

Christ came to build a church of believers that would believe His name and His God, men and women that would be empowered to be inheritors of the kingdom to come, thereby creating a difference between the sheep and the goats, the wheat and the tares, making a difference between the elects and non-elects. God, therefore, reserves the right and power to give to whomsoever he will, the ability to understand the mysteries of the kingdom.

Remember Matthew 13:11? When the mother of Zebedee's children came to Christ asking Him to grant that her two sons be placed on either side of Him, one on the right and the other on His left side, the Lord plainly declares, it's not for Him to decide who sits on either side of Him, but the right of the Father, God Almighty, Himself alone. This is our inheritance.

So the mystery of who gets into heaven is actually not based on personal human efforts, but of God that justifies the ungodly. For righteousness is not attained by works but by grace. For if righteousness be by works, the word of God declares Christ then died in vain. *"I do not frustrate the grace of God: for if righteousness come by the law, then Christ is dead in vain" (Galatians 2:21).*

Then if God alone decides who enters the kingdom, the parable of the rich man and Lazarus spoken by Jesus must not and cannot be taken literally.

THE RICH MAN

Ecclesiastes 9:5–6 states: *"For the living know that they shall die: but the dead know not anything, neither have they any more a reward; for the memory of them is forgotten. Also, their love, and their hatred, and their envy, is now perished; neither have they any more a portion forever in anything that is done under the sun."*

As we have seen in the above scripture, the dead have no more a portion of anything done under the sun and there is no knowledge or device in the grave where they shall reside awaiting resurrection. So, by what means (love) does the rich man advocate compassion for his other brethren spoken about in the parable? By what knowledge did the rich man get to recognize Abraham? If the former things of old cannot be remembered. *"Remember ye not the former things, neither consider the things of old. Behold, I will do a new thing; now it shall spring forth; shall ye not know it? I will even make a way in the wilderness, and rivers in the desert" (Isaiah 43:18–19).*

We cannot stay in blindness of the truth, knowing that the truth alone is what can make us free: free from the oncoming judgment of our righteous King.

When the Bible spoke to us in Luke 16:19 about the rich man that fared sumptuously, clothed in purple and fine linen, Jesus was indirectly talking to groups of peoples that are duly represented in chapter 15 verse 1, in quote, *"The Publican"* and *"Sinners."* The Publicans, who represent the elite group in Israel, and the Sinners which make up the poor and rejected in the land. *"Then drew near unto him all the publicans and sinners for to hear him And the Pharisees and scribes murmured, saying, This man receiveth sinners, and eateth with them" (Luke 15:1–2).* Jesus wasn't interested in the fine linen or the glamour the scribes possessed; he was interested in the lost sheep of the house of Israel. He said in Mark 2:17, *". . . They that are whole have no need of the physician, but they that are sick: I came not to call the righteous, but sinners to repentance".*

The attention Christ was giving to sinners made the super-holy Pharisees jealous. When God is busy fixing our mess, sometimes it causes a stir in the minds of those that feel they are better than us. Then they oppose to our promotion, they stand in the way of our spiritual makeover, but thank God that our God is not a respecter of persons. In Matthew 23:1–3, *"Then spake Jesus to the multitude, and to his disciples, Saying, The scribes and the Pharisees sit in Moses' seat: All therefore whatsoever they bid you know observe, that observe and do; but do not ye after their works: for they say, and do not."* *"But all their works they do for to be seen of men: they make broad their phylacteries, and enlarge the borders of their garments"* (Matthew 23:5).

I am specifically blessed to know the Lord is a compassionate Lord who looks not on the outward of a man, but on the inward. Thank God even so, that God is not man, else the casualty of the downtrodden would have been irrepressible.

The "rich man" in this parable does not necessarily interpret or relate to those who were rich financially or materially only, but to all that display the element of pride, unteachable spirit, and self-willed and uncircumcised individuals claiming to know God but denying the Only Begotten of the Father, Jesus Christ. They are unmerciful, boasters, lovers of pleasures more than lovers of God.

The Pharisees and the high priest were men who were so puffed up and lofty in their spirit. They positioned themselves as the pride of their society. These are those who like to be called names in public places.*"Then spake Jesus to the multitude, and to his disciples, Saying, The scribes and the Pharisees sit in Moses' seat: All therefore whatsoever they bid you observe, that observe and do; but do not ye after their works: for they say, and do not. For they bind heavy burdens and grievous to be borne, and lay them on men's shoulders; but they themselves will not move them with one of their fingers. But all their works they do for to be seen of men: they make broad their phylacteries, and enlarge the borders of their garments, And love the uppermost rooms at feasts, and the chief seats in the synagogues, And greetings in the markets, and to be called of men, Rabbi, Rabbi"* (Matthew 23:1–7).

This is the kind of riches the Lord is referring to in His teaching. Now, with this understanding, let us dive deeper to find the meaning of "The gate, the sores, and the dogs" in reference to the parable.

THE GATE, THE SORES, AND THE DOGS

The Bible says the Pharisees sat on Moses' seat. They had all the beauty of life, they had all comeliness of greatness, but as for the poor they had nothing but suffering; only seeking hope for life. We read that the poor was at the gate of the rich. Have you pondered what in the wildest world could be the meaning of "the gate"? It might amaze you, what the meaning might offer in the understanding of what "gates" are in their synopsis. I am sure you are curious to know like many others.

Jesus said, *"Upon this rock I will build my Church and the Gates of Hell will not prevail against it" (Matthew 16:18).* Well, surprisingly the gates are ministers. This will be explained in further chapters.

The high priests are the rich and are rulers in Israel, the poor aren't. Jesus was not born among the rich or in the house of the high priest in Israel. He was born among the poor and died for them signifying that he represented what he preached and stood for. He also signified that in Matthew 5:3, saying *"Blessed are the poor in spirit, for theirs is the kingdom of God."*

What our Lord Jesus was trying to illustrate in this parable were:

(1) the fact that the rich are those who were at the helm of power; and
(2) the poor were always trampled at their gates waiting on their mercies, on their resources, and whatsoever they had to offer; that was the poor man's provision of salvation. That was their strength of sustenance.

The poor with their sores (infirmities, maladies, weaknesses, and sinfulness) waited at the rich man's (high priest) gates (source of hope to the meek and lowly in spirit) for the crumbs that fell from their tables. The poor waited to receive the mercies of God for their healing. They waited to receive at least a bit of hope for their restoration from the abundance of knowledge of the high priest, the prophets, and the scribes, especially of all they have received from God through their office with God. Rather, all the poor man received was mockery, an ungodly intimidator that laughed at him.

CRUMBS

"Then Jesus went thence, and departed into the coasts of Tyre and Sidon. And behold, a woman of Canaan came out of the same coasts, and cried unto him, saying, Have mercy on me, O Lord, thou Son of David; my daughter is grievously vexed with a devil. But he answered her not a word. And his disciples came and besought him, saying, Send her away; for she crieth after us. But he answered and said, I am not sent but unto the lost sheep of the house of Israel. Then came she and worshipped him, saying, Lord, help me. But he answered and said, It is not meet to take the children's bread, and to cast it to dogs. And she said, Truth, Lord: yet the dogs eat of the crumbs which fall from their masters' table. Then Jesus answered and said unto her, O woman, great is thy faith: be it unto thee even as thou wilt. And her daughter was made whole from that very hour" (Matthew 15:21–28).

Just as the poor does not mean the destitute of the land per se, so too do the crumbs that fell from the master's table. The crumbs do not mean particles of food left over from anyone.

The above passage speaks of a woman who was a Canaanite, whose daughter was grievously vexed with a devil, who asked Jesus for help crying, "Have mercy" (a beggar). Jesus replied, "I was not sent but to the lost sheep of Israel," and the woman stooped down and worshipped him. Yet Jesus said it is not met to give what belongs to the children to dogs.

Jesus typified the Canaanite woman as a dog. Why? Because they valued not the grace of God, neither were they thankful. But let's see the woman's response in verse 27. She said, "Though I know my people are classified as dogs, yet I am asking you to see as my Lord, the dogs do have the right to feed from the crumbs that fall off from the master's table." Meaning: though the Gentiles be unworthy of the benefit of salvation which belongs to the Jews, yet the heathen that be close to the Commonwealth of Israel should not be deprived of the marks of grace and the element of God's provision.

DOGS

The dogs are the base element in the Pharisees' faith, the unsaved Jews that are ignorant of the truth about grace. They are like their masters, the rich, who know no better than to frustrate the grace of God for their lives and those that wait upon them (*Matthew 15:21–28*). Some characteristics of a dog are the tendencies for them to assume the position of leadership which they are not qualified for humanly speaking, but staggers at the good intention of salvation. We might need to review some of the characteristics of a dog in reference to our study of hell.

David gave us a good picture of the activities of the dogs referred to by our Lord, in Psalms 59:1–8, *"To the chief Musician, Altaschith, Michtam of David; when Saul sent, and they watched the house to kill him. Deliver me from mine enemies, O my God: defend me from them that rise up against me. Deliver me from the workers of iniquity, and save me from bloody men. For, lo, they lie in wait for my soul: the mighty are gathered against me; not for my transgression, nor for my sin, O LORD. They run and prepare themselves without my fault: awake to help me, and behold. Thou, therefore, O LORD God of hosts, the God of Israel, awake to visit all the heathen: be not merciful to any wicked transgressors. Selah. They return at evening: they make a noise like a dog, and go round about the city. Behold, they belch out with their mouth: swords are in their lips: for who, say they, doth hear? But thou, O LORD, shalt laugh at them; thou shalt have all the heathen in derision."*

Let us draw attention to the activities of the dogs. Is it possible to forget the mockery the woman with issue of blood for twelve years suffered in the midst of her beholders in Luke 8:43? Or the woman caught in adultery in John 8:4–11? *"They say unto him, Master, this woman was taken in adultery, in the very act. Now Moses in the law commanded us, that such should be stoned: but what sayest thou? This they said, tempting him, that they might have to accuse him. But Jesus stooped down, and with his finger wrote on the ground, as though he heard them not. So when they continued asking him, he lifted up himself, and said unto them, He that is without sin among you, let him first cast a stone at her. And again, he stooped down, and wrote on the ground. And they which heard it, being convicted by their own conscience, went out one by one, beginning at the eldest, even unto the last: and Jesus was left alone, and the woman standing in the midst. When Jesus had lifted up himself, and saw none but the woman, he said unto her, Woman, where are those thine accusers? hath no man condemned thee? She said, No man, Lord. And Jesus said unto her, Neither do I condemn thee: go, and sin no more."*

And the man in the synagogue that hath the spirit of an unclean devil: *"And in the synagogue there was a man, which had a spirit of an unclean devil, and cried out with a loud voice, Saying, Let us alone; what have we to do with thee, thou Jesus of Nazareth? art thou come to destroy us? I know thee who thou art; the Holy One of God. And Jesus rebuked him, saying, Hold thy peace, and come out of him. And when the devil had thrown him in the midst, he came out of him, and hurt him not. And they were all amazed, and spake among themselves, saying, What a word is this! for with authority and power he commandeth the unclean spirits, and they come out"* (Luke 4:33–36).

Neither can any forget the Bethesda man who was at the pool for thirty-eight years under five porches, which supposing, should represent a form of covering or a type of the five-fold ministry! *"After this there was a feast of the Jews; and Jesus went up to Jerusalem. Now there is at Jerusalem by the sheep market a pool, which is called in the Hebrew tongue*

Bethesda, having five porches. In these lay a great multitude of impotent folk, of blind, halt, withered, waiting for the moving of the water. For an angel went down at a certain season into the pool, and troubled the water: whosoever then first after the troubling of the water stepped in was made whole of whatsoever disease he had. And a certain man was there, which had an infirmity thirty and eight years. When Jesus saw him lie, and knew that he had been now a long time in that case, he saith unto him, Wilt thou be made whole? The impotent man answered him, Sir, I have no man, when the water is troubled, to put me into the pool: but while I am coming, another steppeth down before me. Jesus saith unto him, Rise, take up thy bed, and walk. And immediately the man was made whole, and took up his bed, and walked: and on the same day was the sabbath" (John 5:1–9).

Where was the high priest that was in charge at the temple? Or the prophets that were supposed to be watchmen over God's heritage? Those poor men (Lazarus and others) waited to no avail until their Jesus, the Good Shepherd came and turn their captivity around.

I feel something good is coming your way! Keep on pressing in and pressing on; it will not be too long before our Redeemer will visit you at the point of your needs.

"And great multitudes came unto him, having with them those that were lame, blind, dumb, maimed, and many others, and cast them down at Jesus' feet; and he healed them: Insomuch that the multitude wondered, when they saw the dumb to speak, the maimed to be whole, the lame to walk, and the blind to see: and they glorified the God of Israel" (Matthew 15:30–31).

The dogs are those who, out of ignorance worked their whole life after self-righteousness. They frustrate the grace of God and make of no reputation the salvation of the Lord Christ. Jesus counseled the apostles of his day saying, "Give not that which is holy to dogs." *"Give not that which is holy unto the dogs, neither cast ye your pearls before swine, lest they trample them under their feet, and turn again and rend you"* (Matthew 7:6).

THE BEGGAR

While we dig deeper into the understanding of the parable of the rich man and Lazarus, it is necessary to establish the understanding that the *beggar* does not necessarily place a reference to finances as in reference to poverty in layman's terms. Oh no!

The poor in Spirit are men that follow Christ to whatever extent he required of them to go. They obeyed, submitted, and are never offended at what the Lord commands them to do. *"Blessed are the poor in spirit: for theirs is the kingdom of heaven"(Matthew 5:3).*

The beggar in this passage is in reference to the poor as it is written in 1 Samuel 2:8. The beggars are men and women that are poor and probably unable to meet their personal needs such as healings, miracles, and the gift of life.

When the disciples asked who was to be greatest in heaven, Christ responded with this answer in Matthew 18:1–4, *"At the same time came the disciples unto Jesus, saying, Who is the greatest in the kingdom of heaven? And Jesus called a little child unto him, and set him in the midst of them, And said, Verily I say unto you, Except ye be converted, and become as little children, ye shall not enter into the kingdom of heaven. Whosoever therefore shall humble himself as this little child, the same is greatest in the kingdom of heaven."*

The poor are likened to helpless little children's mentality of understanding.

Lazarus in this parable was considered a beggar showing us he had not what life has to offer. He was depraved and considered a scorn of the earth in every standard, but God promised something good in return for his inability. *"Hearken, my beloved brethren, Hath not God chosen the poor of this world rich in faith, and heirs of the kingdom which he hath promised to them that love him?" (James 2:5).* What a privilege to be offered a kingdom in place of the vanity of this life.

Jesus shows us whom He refers to as poor in the presence of God and in His words: *"Blessed are the poor in spirit: for theirs is the kingdom of heaven" (Matthew 5:3).*

Just for a quick sense of reasoning, Ananias and Sapphira were not poor to have a house to sell, in order to assist the disciples in their ministry *(Acts 5:1)*. Barnabas who was surnamed José's the son of Consolation *(Acts. 4:36)* couldn't have been considered poor to be a kingdom financier in his day. Neither were the apostles mere fishermen that rob nickel with nickel in order to make ends meet. If this be so, Christ would not have been woken up from the lower arch of the fishing boat where he was asleep. If all they had was a mere simple canoe or boat, only to be woken up by the Apostle in the event of the storm, which Jesus rose up to rebuke in Mark 4:37–39, *"And there arose a great storm of wind, and the waves beat into the ship, so that it was now full. And he was in the hinder part of the ship, asleep on a pillow: and they awake him, and say unto him, Master, carest thou not that we perish? And he arose, and rebuked the wind, and said unto the sea, Peace, be still. And the wind ceased, and there was a great calm."*

They were men of wealth. They had what it took to build an enterprise. They had a fishing trawler to show for it. They had a place below deck level where Jesus laid. So, by no means were the disciples poor as many purposed in their thought.

The "poor" Jesus was talking about in the scripture were the poor in the spirit, the lowly, the gentle, not because they couldn't fight, but because of Christ, they suffered all things that they may attain unto the power of His resurrection. The point in the classification of the "poor" is in this wise; no one had to be poor to be able to make heaven or enter into the soon-coming Kingdom of our Lord and Savior Jesus Christ. In other words, the beggar being poor, hath no chance with the rich so-called. They are always prey to the rich who hath no mercy. *"There is a generation, O how lofty are their eyes! and their eyelids are lifted up. There is a generation, whose teeth are as swords, and their jaw teeth as* knives, to devour the poor from off the earth, and the needy from among men" (Proverbs 30:13–14).

THE BOSOM

In Luke 16:22, there is a line of thought that might interest us sufficiently enough to command our focus. The scripture that says both the rich man and the poor beggar died, and an angel did carry the poor man to Abraham's bosom, while the rich man was buried. In verse 23, the rich man being in hell cried out. *"And it came to pass, that the beggar died, and was carried by the angels into Abraham's bosom: the rich man also died, and was buried; And in hell he lift up his eyes, being in torments, and seeth Abraham afar off, and Lazarus in his bosom" (Luke 16:22–23).*

Wait a minute! What if we are to consider this thought more appropriately in a literal sense, the rich man was buried in hell. Signifying once again that hell is grave! When a man dies, he is buried in the grave, tomb, or sepulcher. No one buries their loved ones in fiery flame, even those that practice or approve cremation. What they get in return is dust or ashes. Not even the men who bound the three Hebrew children escaped the scorching heat of the flame in King Nebuchadnezzar's days.

So, for this rich man to be tormented and needed the poor man to dip his finger in water and cool his thirst, a man who also is in the grave (hell) as himself!

We need the Holy Spirit to help us understand this parable, and to find out evidently what hell is. *"Marvel not at this: for the hour is coming, in the which all that are in the graves shall hear his voice, And shall come forth; they that have done good, unto the resurrection of life; and they that have done evil, unto the resurrection of damnation" (John 5:28–29).*

The parable did not speak of the rich man in hell hearing the voice of Christ, but rather, they that are in the grave. So, if this is not in the parable, how was this rich man able to communicate with Lazarus who supposedly is in Abraham's bosom?

There is a universal acclaim that all that are of the faith are the seed of Abraham *(Isaiah 51:2; Romans 4:1)*. How shall we be Abraham's seed without coming from his bosom? *(Gen 15: 5–6)*.

The paternity of a child is defined by the father's DNA or genes. In other words, when the scripture says that Lazarus was carried to Abraham's bosom, it means that Abraham who lived by faith through God whom he believed, was the symbol of the poor in spirit of all believers. He suffered persecution, he was mocked by many, he was afflicted like many, but believed in God in spite of it all. So, it became obvious that when Lazarus died, it will be said that he fell asleep with his fathers. In other words, as Abraham lived and died in the faith, so likewise, Lazarus lived and died in the faith as Father Abraham. And so, as the father of all faithful, all who abide in faith are ambiguous, which is the right words used in describing God's faithful in their final walk with God. See the following scriptures: 1 Kings 2:10, *"So David slept with his fathers, and was buried in the city of David."* 1 Kings 11:43, *"And Solomon slept with his fathers, and was buried in the city of David his father: and Rehoboam his son reigned in his stead."* 1 Kings 14:3, *"And Rehoboam slept with his fathers, and was buried with his fathers in the city of David. And his mother's name was Naamah an Ammonitess. And Abijam his son reigned in his stead."* 1 Kings 15:8, *"And Abijam slept with his fathers; and they buried him in the city of David: and Asa his son reigned in his stead."* 1 Kings 22:50, *"And Jehoshaphat slept with his fathers, and was buried with his fathers in the city of David his father: and Jehoram his son reigned in his stead."*

Lazarus did not live by the law, he had no power to live by the law. He probably never had enough all through his time to buy the rams for daily sacrifice for sins. He was a man who solely depended on God. Lazarus could not live by the food from the table of the rich man according to the parable. What table could the Bible be talking about? If not the banqueting of the two tables of stones of the laws given to Moses by God which if a man should live by, He shall be blessed, but how many have been able to keep it perfectly from youth? *"For the promise, that he should be the heir of the world, was not to Abraham, or to his seed, through the law, but through the righteousness of faith. For if they which are of the law be heirs, faith is made void, and the promise made of none effect: Because the law worketh wrath: for where no law is, there is no transgression. Therefore it is of faith, that it might be by grace; to the end the promise might be sure to all the seed; not to that only which is of the law, but to that also which is of the faith of Abraham; who is the father of us all, (As it is written, I have made thee a father of many nations,) before him whom he believed, even God, who quickeneth the dead, and calleth those things which be not as though they were. Who against hope believed in hope, that he might become the father of many nations, according to that which was spoken, So shall thy seed be"* (Romans 4:13–18).

Abraham hoped against hope, he exhausted his strength in waiting for the Lord yet he hoped on still. He kept hope alive thereby becoming the father of us all. Though he was rich in earthly goods yet was poor in spirit, trust, and leaning on the Lord for salvation. Lazarus, like Abraham, lived with God by faith, believed God by faith. Lazarus in the parable could only be referred to as one on Abraham's bosom, because unlike the Jews who trusted in their laws, Abraham was not Jewish. For a Jewish is one who feels he is called, or chosen by God, but ends up holding to the law rather than Christ, who paid the penalty for sin, to them who were under the law.

Hence the Bible says if any man thinks in keeping the law, he shall be made perfect and righteous before God, then such a one has not known the scriptures. See Galatians 2:16, *"Knowing that a man is not justified by the works of the law, but by the faith of Jesus Christ, even we have believed in Jesus Christ, that we might be justified by the faith of Christ, and not by the works of the law: for by the works of the law shall no flesh be justified."* In Galatians 2:21, Apostle Paul declared, *"I do not frustrate the grace of God: for if righteousness come by the law, then Christ is dead in vain."*

A rich young man approached Christ concerning entering the kingdom of God based on his merits in Matthew 19:16–22: *"And, behold, one came and said unto him, Good Master, what good thing shall I do, that I may have eternal life? And he said unto him, Why callest thou me good? there is none good but one, that is, God: but if thou wilt enter into life, keep the commandments. He saith unto him, Which? Jesus said, Thou shalt do no murder, Thou shalt not commit adultery, Thou shalt not steal, Thou shalt not bear false witness, Honour thy father and thy mother: and, Thou shalt love thy neighbour as thyself. The young man saith unto him, All these things have I kept from my youth up: what lack I yet? Jesus said unto him, If thou wilt be perfect, go and sell that thou hast, and give to the poor, and thou shalt have treasure in heaven: and come and follow me. But when the young man heard that saying, he went away sorrowful: for he had great possessions."*

From the above scripture in Matthew 19, the young man in keeping the law thought he must have arrived at his full potential of being a candidate of the kingdom by keeping the law, until he was asked to go and sell all he had and give it to the poor. This he couldn't do because he had great possessions. His riches held him back from the Lord. He was RICH in the law (Jew), but poor in grace, poor in spirit. Notice in the scriptures, he couldn't reach out to the poor. He couldn't give what he had to the poor in spirit. He could not share the mercies he had, because of his riches. Right there, he frustrated the grace of God upon his life by putting confidence upon the law, rather than in the Messiah. The law which the weak and the poor could not keep or afford, because of the fallibility of the flesh and insufficiencies on their part, Christ came in likeness of the flesh and paid the price that the poor could not pay. So, like Abraham that believed in God that justifies the ungodly, so are the poor in their own little way believed in the coming of the Messiah for a better hope.

TABLE

The table from which crumbs fell, only carries a little amount of grace, or mercy, showing us that at the time of the law, grace was extremely limited to the reach of the few who dare believe in the Lord Jesus Christ. The beggar had no knowledge of the saving grace of God. He fed off from the little mercy that the law offers. The Bible tells us the law came by Moses, but grace came by the Lord Jesus Christ. The law was "an eye for an eye." Christ had to come and save us and all those that were downtrodden in Israel from such impending danger by bringing in charity that covers a multitude of sins. *"And above all things have fervent charity among yourselves: for charity shall cover the multitude of sins"* (1 Peter 4:8). *"And the LORD said unto Moses, Come up to me into the mount, and be there: and I will give thee tables of stone, and a law, and commandments which I have written; that thou mayest teach them"* (Exodus 24:12). *"And he gave unto Moses, when he had made an end of communing with him upon mount Sinai, two tables of testimony, tables of stone, written with the finger of God"* (Exodus 31:18).

The rich man's table was not a literal table. Again, because the narrative is a parable, not a reality. The "table" was the table of stone upon which the laws were written. Literally, a stone cannot be ingested as a parchment or paper which John was commanded to eat. For the Lord asked John to eat: *"And the voice which I heard from heaven spake unto me again, and said, Go and take the little book which is open in the hand of the angel which standeth upon the sea and upon the earth. And I went unto the angel, and said unto him, Give me the little book. And he said unto me, Take it, and eat it up; and it shall make thy belly bitter, but it shall be in thy mouth sweet as honey. And I took the little book out of the angel's hand, and ate it up; and it was in my mouth sweet as honey: and as soon as I had eaten it, my belly was bitter"* (Revelation 10:8–10).

So, the question that might arise from this train of thought will be, why will God write the law on a stone? What will be the significance of a stone scroll? The answer is: because God knew man cannot keep the law unto salvation, something they could never ingest, hence the need of a Savior. The Bible tells me the law was as a schoolmaster, which was to point us to Christ. *"But before faith came, we were kept under the law, shut up unto the faith which should afterwards be revealed. Wherefore the law was our schoolmaster to bring us unto Christ, that we might be justified by faith. But after that faith is come, we are no longer under a schoolmaster. For ye are all the children of God by faith in Christ Jesus"* (Galatians 3:23–26).

For Christ is the end of the law to them that believe. *"Brethren, my heart's desire and prayers to God for Israel is, that they might be saved. For I bear them record that they have a zeal of God, but not according to knowledge. For they being ignorant of God's righteousness, and going about to establish their own righteousness, have not submitted themselves unto the righteousness of God. For Christ is the end of the law for righteousness to everyone that believeth"* (Romans 10:1–4).

But Israel claiming to know God, denied Christ to their own conceit, making themselves richer in the word of God than any nation, by holding unto stony scroll. This is why the rich man cannot make it. Israel would not make it if caution would not be taken.

THE DIP OF COOL WATER

In looking at Luke 16:24, the rich man is seeking mercy, though verse 22 says that they were both dead, but permit me to declare that this was not a literal physical death. Read Ephesians 2:1, *"And you hath he quickened, who were dead in trespasses and sins."* May the Lord quicken our minds to function in His grace in Jesus' name.

If we look at the story of Nicodemus which Christ showed us in John 3:1–10, holding Nicodemus as a type of the rich Pharisees in Israel and Christ representing Father Abraham. Nicodemus came to Jesus saying have mercy on us and show us what we might do to be saved.

Just as Peter, James and John are (a type of Lazarus). He demanded to know how to survive in the hard crucial event of his time. He is seeing that Lazarus (believers) no longer had sores, and no longer begged for the good things of God. He saw Peter, James, John, and the rest of the disciples are secured and safe. *"And the disciples of John and of the Pharisees used to fast: and they come and say unto him, Why do the disciples of John and of the Pharisees fast, but thy disciples fast not? And Jesus said unto them, Can the children of the bridechamber fast, while the bridegroom is with them? As long as they have the bridegroom with them, they cannot fast."*

The scriptures are clear: the rich man (high priest, Pharisees) who fared sumptuously in the past, now wants what Lazarus got. Notice how he said the disciples (followers) of John, and of the Pharisees usually go hungry and wait until they received what is offered to them by the high priest, how now are your followers (disciples) not doing the same? The rich man is thirsty now and the Lord as a type of our Father Abraham asked him, "You want some water?" *"But whosoever drinketh of the water that I shall give him shall never thirst; but the water that I shall give him shall be in him a well of water springing up into everlasting life"* (John 4:14).

"Then will I sprinkle clean water upon you, and ye shall be clean: from all your filthiness, and from all your idols, will I cleanse you. A new heart also will I give you, and a new spirit will I put within you: and I will take away the stony heart out of your flesh, and I will give you a heart of flesh" (Ezekiel 36:25–26).

The dip of cool water is the word of God mixed with the Spirit of God. The WORD which the Lord says, they are Spirit and they are Life (*John 6:63*). Jesus said, out of your belly shall flow the rivers of living waters. He told Nicodemus what you ask for shall require you to be born again, meaning you must be born of water and of the Spirit (*John, 3:3, 5*).

Again, in Ezekiel 37:12–14, *"Therefore prophesy and say unto them, Thus saith the Lord GOD; Behold, O my people, I will open your graves, and cause you to come up out of your graves, and bring you into the land of*

Israel. And ye shall know that I am the LORD, when I have opened your graves, O my people, and brought you up out of your graves, And shall put my spirit in you, and ye shall live, and I shall place you in your own land: then shall ye know that I the LORD have spoken it, and performed it, saith the LORD."

What is the grave being referred to here?

The children of Israel were dead. They were dead out of the presence of God. They were spiritually dead. The valley of dry bones in Ezekiel 37 was a revival call to the house of Israel to come to repentance.

Lazarus was dead, the rich man also was dead, and they are both children of Israel, they both needed the bosom of Abraham. They both needed the faith of Abraham. The bosom of Abraham can only be attainable by faith and the finished product of faith by Christ (father of Abraham). Jesus will produce to us and the children of Israel, the baptism of the Holy Spirit. An internal revival, which will shake all things within and re-establish the need of eternal redemption, which is the only way to the kingdom of God.

You cannot have the baptism of the Holy Ghost by the works of the law except by faith. Every one believer today, needs something that will quench the thirst for righteousness, and sure as it may be, only the Holy Spirit can quench such a thirst and hunger even as Jesus Christ said: *"Blessed are those that thirst and hunger for righteousness they shall be satisfied" (Matthew 5:6).*

THE GREAT GULF

In the 25th verse of chapter 16 of the book of Luke, *"But Abraham said, Son, remember that thou in thy lifetime receivedst thy good things, and likewise Lazarus evil things: but now he is comforted, and thou art tormented."* Do you know how comforting grace could be? You will remember, no matter how great a man's afflictions could be, the Lord has promised to deliver him from them all. Sometimes the wicked get so blessed to the point that they make ridicule of the poor. There be they that assume that those that are rich are of God, while those that are not so rich are considered cursed. I am sure you know this assertion is not entirely true. The poor also are of God (speaking literally). *"He that hath pity upon the poor lendeth unto the LORD; and that which he hath given will he pay him again" (Proverbs 19:17).*

There is a gulf between you and us, Abraham said, according to the parable. The great gulf signifies the 1,900 years that the Children of Israel have been separated and disconnected from God their source, the fountain of life, from the lineage of God, and even from their bloodline. In other words, those that are on that side of the work of God (Old Testament) cannot cross over to this dispensation of grace to partake of the Holy Spirit. So also, those that have received the Holy Spirit now, cannot go backward to start living by the law which the Bible tells us in Hebrews 7:19, *"For the law made nothing perfect, but the bringing in of a better hope did; by the which we draw nigh unto God."*

This why Jesus in talking about John the Baptist, said, *"For I say unto you, among those that are born of women there is not a greater prophet than John the Baptist: but he that is least in the kingdom of God is greater than he" (Luke 7:28)*—showing the mark of the great gulf from the time of John the Baptist to the days of the prophet; enacting also the time between the era of grace and that of the law. There is a great gap of reformation; Moses, right from Sinai where he got the tables of stones, the Jews never ceased feeding from that table. The table of the law which has only a remnant of faith or grace, really has no place or provision for the poor in spirit among the Jewish religion. This was the table that Lazarus did pick the crumbs of faith from before the coming of the dispensing of grace. Now that grace has come with the giving of the Holy Ghost (rivers of living waters) is like life from the dead.

So, in the parable of the rich man and Lazarus, asking that Abraham (father of faith) give justification to those working the law, was an unimaginable request. It is written, *"for by the works of the law shall no flesh be justified"* (*Galatians 2:16b*). Moreover, for the poor (who walked by faith) to come to the platform of the teaching, the rich (who has walked in their life by the law), the measure of the right spirit, the liberty that is in grace, or the anointing that is of the Holy Spirit, was an incomprehensible mystery and challenge in righteousness, except to those who the hand of God has drawn unto Christ, who will evidently be saved.

So, from when Israel doubted the prophets to when Christ came, was almost 1,900 years. Even with Jesus coming to give them the water of life, it was hard for the Jews to accept, and neither could they digest it. Therefore, Jesus spoke to them in parables. John came talking to the people about water baptism, and the Lord came fulfilling all righteousness by water baptism, yet the Jews of His day refused to go into baptism, either literally or spiritually.

Looking back on history, the earth is only 6,000 years young if I may say. After the first 2,000 years, the Lord destroyed the earth with water. If we go back to the book of Genesis and calculate from the beginning to the time of Noah, we see it was about 2,000 years. From the days of Noah to the coming of the Lord was another 2,000 years. It will interest us to know as Noah survived the flood so also the children of Israel all passed through the Red Sea which is a symbol of baptism. *"Moreover, brethren, I would not that ye should be ignorant, how that all our fathers were under the cloud, and all passed through the sea; And were all baptized unto Moses in the cloud and in the sea"* (*1 Corinthians 10:1–4*).

Thereafter, there was nothing mentioned again of baptism in the history of Israel, creating a great gulf between the prophets and the era of Christ the Messiah; and in the coming of John the Baptist who with the voice of a forerunner, challenged Israel to repentance and to true baptism. That was to help prepare the way of the Lord! *"Then went out to him Jerusalem, and all Judaea, and all the region round about Jordan, And were baptized of him in Jordan, confessing their sins. But when he saw many of the Pharisees and Sadducees come to his baptism, he said unto them, O generation of vipers, who hath warned you to flee from the wrath to come? Bring forth therefore fruits meet for repentance: And think not to say within yourselves, We have Abraham to our father: for I say unto you, that God is able of these stones to raise up children unto Abraham"* (Matthew 3:5–9).

This was the heavenly call to the children of God, who, after their loss in self-righteousness, negated their understanding that the clarity of baptism was not just a New Testament order, but has been one of God's great ordinances for revival and salvation. The Bible said, "Abraham told the rich man: If you and your brethren genuinely want some of this water, you need to go back to what the prophets did. You need to go back to the practice of communion and the conversion at baptism."

In being conversant with the Old Testament, you remember the manna that fell from heaven? That manna was a form of spiritual meat that God gave His people to eat and caused them all to drink from the waters of Meribah, which again, is a type of spiritual drink from Christ. For the rock that followed them, which Moses struck, and water gushed out for the children to drink, was Christ. This rock the Bible tells us followed them through the wilderness. *"And did all eat the same spiritual meat; And did all drink the same spiritual drink: for they drank of that spiritual Rock that followed them: and that Rock was Christ"* (1 Corinthians 10:3–4).

It is amazing how the scriptures were written for our learning; that through patience and comfort of the scripture, we might have hope.

Yes, they ate of that manna from heaven because it was sent from God Himself. They drank of that spiritual drink that comes from the Rock of Ages. They enjoyed the union of fellowship which was needed for them to be one with the Lord. They enjoyed partnership with the Lord at that time. The Lord was their stay, their refuge, their fortress.

Except for those who stood in rebellion and died the death of fools in the wilderness, those who adhered to the truth of the word stayed alive; they entered into their inheritance. They were fulfilled such as Joshua and Caleb who earned the Lord's blessing to enter into their inheritance because they followed Him wholly (*Deuteronomy 1:35–38*).

Before the Lord Jesus departed this earth, He commanded that the communion must be maintained because it is the union of mankind with the Lord their Maker (*Luke 22:17–19*). The importance of the communion, water baptism, and the infilling of the Holy Spirit, cannot be over-emphasized. The Lord needed man to find his root back to eternity by simple obedience. The salvation of the Jews or Gentiles depends on the sanctified obedience of their faith and commitment to the things of righteousness. Christ was literally teaching in this parable what we need to do to inherit the fullness of the kingdom, by staying in the obedience of baptism and the fellowship of his suffering being the covenant and the bond between us our Redeemer (*Hebrews 8:6–13*).

Jesus said, *"If ye eat of my flesh and drink of my blood then and only then will you have life"* (*John 6:53–57*). If a man dies without Christ on the inside, they will resurrect to face crises.

Had it not been for the Lord, what would have been left of humanity? The restarting of the baptism became a lifeline. Jesus came and entered into a covenant by re-establishing the act of baptism of water and of fire again, so that man in their carnality will not perish without hope. He said, "Except man be born again, he cannot enter the kingdom." Yet, many in their status had no idea where lies their salvation; not even Nicodemus the ruler of the Jews in his day.

So, in the account of Nicodemus, Jesus turned to him, a representative of the Pharisees, saying unto him, "Art thou become so rich and know not how to quench your thirst, has thou been a ruler in Israel and knoweth not these things (how to get saved)?" *"Marvel not that I said unto thee, Ye must be born again. The wind bloweth where it listeth, and thou hearest the sound thereof, but canst not tell whence it cometh, and whither it goeth: so is every one that is born of the Spirit. Nicodemus answered and said unto him, How can these things be? Jesus answered and said unto him, Art thou a master of Israel, and knowest not these things?"* (John 3:7–10).

Though Nicodemus had been a ruler in Israel yet he needed the water of sanctification and the fire of purification to be able to experience the power of the Kingdom that is soon to be established. With Nicodemus' encounter with Jesus, everything goes on to show it is not enough to be in church, engulfed in sacrificial activities. Without knowing how to get saved is a dangerous thing. It is quite unfortunate that a man can be in church, or circular religion, and still be lost. Isn't that something? As I have always told many individuals, Christ did not come to die for the church you go to. He came to die for the church in you. In you, He is building a church, a sanctuary of hope.

Oh, to God we will all take heed to our calling!

If not for the mercies of God, Nicodemus would have died in his ignorance believing he's saved, serving the Lord. May the Lord open our eyes to behold the course of our destiny.

THE FIVE BRETHREN

Luke 16:27–28, *"Then he said, I pray thee therefore, father, that thou wouldest send him to my father's house: For I have five brethren; that he may testify unto them, lest they also come into this place of torment."* In the above scriptures, we see a request being made, asking Abraham to dispatch messengers to the rich man's father's house by the rich man himself, which in interpretation is the house of Israel with a message to his FIVE BRETHREN.

Well, who could these brethren be? I am sure it will be interesting to find out. Jesus speaking in this parable, foreseeing the house of Israel in disarray, spoke of the children of Israel who are divided and scattered among the nations. These nations were powers in world history. These nations were Babylon, Assyria, Media-Persia, Greece, and pagan Rome. The five brethren that the rich man was referring to, were those Jews that were scattered among these nations. While each of these powers ruled the world in their dispensation, they in some ways did affect the house of Israel either by captivity, trade, or by posterity to where the hearts of many of the Jews were led astray from serving the true God. Many of these beloved sons and daughters of Israel were lured into captivity—human captivity, or mental slavery. Many of them sojourned in foreign nations for the benefit of advantages and, some for self-inflicted hardship and sorrow. Many remain in ignorance, practicing their Jewish religion—Judaism, of which within itself can never bring man salvation.

Paul in referencing them mentioned it in Romans 10:1–4, *"Brethren, my heart's desire and prayer to God for Israel is, that they might be saved. For I bear them record that they have a zeal of God, but not according to knowledge. For they being ignorant of God's righteousness, and going about to establish their own righteousness, have not submitted themselves unto the righteousness of God. For Christ is the end of the law for righteousness to everyone that believeth"*.

The request of the rich man concerning his brethren was to see them recovered from the wrath of the law, which is a curse to them who live thereby. For the scripture says: Christ has redeemed us from the curse of the law. So, if the human race has been redeemed from the curse of the law, it was obvious the rich man does not want to see himself as a defeat to the purpose of God with his brothers inclusive. The reward which he has seen in the life of the poor Lazarus, who was already attaining it in Christ Jesus. The poor (Lazarus) who possibly had no choice but to receive the extended grace of God stands to benefit this purpose of true salvation through faith. Knowing that only by the gift of God one can be saved through faith (*Ephesians 2:8–9*).

Each of these powers has ruled the world successively in their days and possibly held the Jews in captivity, or ruled over those that migrated to their nation for the purpose of commerce and trade, or abject captivity. Regardless of the status of these Jews, they were still deemed to be God's children. These, the rich man considered, deserved to know the word of truth that relates to their salvation, so that they do not get involved in the impending judgments that await those who will refuse the mercies of the Lord for their salvation. *"And to you who are troubled rest with us, when the Lord Jesus shall be revealed from heaven with his mighty angels, In flaming fire taking vengeance on them that know not God, and that obey not the gospel of our Lord Jesus Christ: Who shall be punished with everlasting destruction from the presence of the Lord, and from the glory of his power; When he shall come to be glorified in his saints, and to be admired in all them that believe (because our testimony among you was believed) in that day"* (2 Thessalonians 1:7–10).

The response of Abraham to the rich man in the parable was simple: *"Abraham saith unto him, they have Moses and the prophets; let them hear them. And he said, nay, Father Abraham: but if one went unto them from the dead, they would repent. And he said unto him, If they hear not Moses and the prophets, neither will they be persuaded, though one rose from the dead"* (Luke 16:29–31).

Abraham said to him they have Moses and the prophets let them hear them, meaning: they have these faithful men who did speak of the coming of the Messiah and eminent deliverance that was to liberate the people of God from spiritual bondage and captivity. Should they (five brethren), hear the truth of the gospel which evidently sterns from the Old Testament to the New, they will surely get saved. Likewise, today if we on this side of the work of creation should hearken to the truth of the gospel, then, we shall likewise be saved as so the Jews.

7

What is the Gate of Hell?

The Gate of Hell is like many other gates, leads in, or leads out. In Mathew 16:18, Jesus Christ the Great Redeemer states, *"And I say also unto thee, that thou are Peter, and upon this rock I will build my church; and the gates of hell shall not prevail against it."* The big question here will be what could the gate of hell possibly be? Of course, many religious organizations have cast their views and interpretations over the idea that Peter could be the rock, when in reality it is the Lord Jesus Christ who is the rock. The holy rites declare that no prophecy of the scriptures is of any private interpretation. *"Knowing this first, that no prophecy of the scripture is of any private interpretation. For the prophecy came not in old time by the will of man: but holy men of God spake as they were moved by the Holy Ghost"* (2 Peter 1:20–21).

For the benefit of those who may have been misinformed that Peter is the rock by an organized religion, it would be right for us to point to Psalms 18:31, *"For who is God save the LORD? or who is a rock save our God."* Paul likewise spoke of Christ in like manner as the Rock in 1 Corinthians 10:1–4 saying, *"Moreover, brethren, I would not that ye should be ignorant, how that all our fathers were under the cloud, and all passed through the sea; And were all baptized unto Moses in the cloud and in the sea; And did all eat the same spiritual meat; And did all drink the same spiritual drink: for they drank of that spiritual Rock that followed them: and that Rock was Christ."*

Without controversy, it will be a wise intent to accept the truth of who the rock is and who has always been the rock. *"The LORD is my rock, and my fortress, and my deliverer; my God, my strength, in whom I will trust; my buckler, and the horn of my salvation, and my high tower"* (Psalms 18:2).

So, it is obvious that everyone should know who the rock is, on which the church is going to be built, that is the Christ, who represents the Word of God. The church will be built upon the Word of God, Christ, not Peter. *"And he was clothed with a vesture dipped in blood: and his name is called The Word of God"* (Revelation 19:13).

But now back to the main subject matter, what did Christ mean when He said that the gates of hell shall not prevail against the building of His church? To fully understand what He meant, one must first understand why He came in the first place.

In Isaiah 61:1, a definite explanation is given, *"The Spirit of the Lord GOD is upon me; because the LORD hath anointed me to preach good tidings unto the meek; he hath sent ME to BIND UP the BROKENHEARTED, to PROCLAIM LIBERTY to the CAPTIVES, and the OPENING of the PRISON to them that are BOUND."*

To start with, a person can be held captive by Satan, their mind, and even imprisoned by both. In other words, when they are bound, they are in bondage.

What this means is, that a person's MIND can be held CAPTIVE and even IMPRISONED within the four walls of their own heads by Satan, or by what they give reason to believe. The word of God says in 2 Corinthians 10:4–6, *"For the weapons of our warfare are not carnal, but mighty through God to the pulling down of strong holds; Casting down imaginations, and every high thing that exalteth itself against the knowledge of God, and bringing into captivity every thought to the obedience of Christ;*

And having in a readiness to revenge all disobedience when your obedience is fulfilled."

Now should anyone be in prison, the only way out must be through the gates of the four-walled units. I mean, if the gate to the prison cell is not open, then the fact is, the person in the cell will stay and remain imprisoned, they will remain a captive, in bondage.

Now, having a full understanding of the concept being used, the four walls of one's own head could represent a prison cell. In this prison cell lies one's mind. Therefore, for anyone's mind to become free from such bondage, the person in question must first open the gate of the prison cell. Permit me to say the gate of that prison is one's mouth.

The mouth undoubtedly represents the gate of the prison cell called the four walls of one's own head. Once we open the gate and proclaim the truth out of it, then and only are we no longer captives of Satan, but will actually be free in Christ, as written in John 8:32, *"And ye shall know the truth, and the truth shall make you free."*

For those that have not grasped the definition of one's mouth as a gate, please look at Proverbs 17:18–20, *"A man void of understanding striketh hands, and becometh surety in the presence of his friend. He loveth transgression that loveth strife: and he that exalteth his gate seeketh destruction. He that hath a froward heart findeth no good: and he that hath a perverse tongue falleth into mischief."*

Here it is plain that the term gate means one's mouth. I want everyone to fully understand what Christ meant when He said of His church, that the gates/mouths of hell shall not prevail against it.

Now to take this a bit deeper, in the Old Testament, the prophets of God would stand in the gate of the actual temple of God and proclaim to the people to repent and to turn back to God and keep His commandments. *"Yet the LORD testified against Israel, and against Judah, by all the prophets, and by all the seers, saying, Turn ye from your evil ways, and keep my commandments and my statutes, according to all the law which I commanded your fathers, and which I sent to you by my servants the prophets"* (2 Kings 17:13).

But now there is no physical building that a prophet can stand in and proclaim the Truth of God, as it has been destroyed not once, but twice. Please understand, a temple has a gate, and now that temple is our own physical bodies. *"Know ye not that ye are the temple of God, and that the Spirit of God dwelleth in you?" (1 Corinthians 3:16).*

If a person's body represents the temple of God, then that same individual's mouth represents the gate of that temple by which God speaks to one, or to all, regardless of who, when, or where they stand in their faith. What really matters is what is proclaimed out of that gate. *"Death and Life is in the power of the tongue" (Proverbs 19:21)*. This is necessary to our understanding because the truth that sets one free only comes from the mouth/gate when spoken. Furthermore, the scripture declares, the only tool to help man achieve his purpose with God must first be spoken for it to take effect. Here is how it goes, *"Faith cometh by Hearing and hearing by the word of God" (Romans 10:17).*

For one to truly become free, they must have their broken heart repaired, and that is the reason Christ came, to bind up the brokenhearted. *"He that committeth sin is of the devil; for the devil sinneth from the beginning. For this purpose, the Son of God was manifested, that he might destroy the works of the devil" (1 John 3:8)*. This is so important because of what Christ taught. He taught that from the abundance of the heart the mouth speaks. *"A good man out of the good treasure of his heart bringeth forth that which is good; and an evil man out of the evil treasure of his heart bringeth forth that which is evil: for of the abundance of the heart his mouth speaketh" (Luke 6:45).*

Only if a person allows his heart to be repaired and healed, then, can such one begin to proclaim the truth out of their gate. Once that happens, the truth of God from that soul causes him, or her, to no longer be bound; they no longer remain captives; they are no longer held imprisoned. They start to enjoy freedom from sin and death. They no more are snared nor taken captive by the words they speak. *"Thou art snared with the words of thy mouth, thou art taken with the words of thy mouth" (Proverbs 6:2).*

So, what Christ meant when He said the gates of hell shall not prevail against the building of His church, He meant the tongue that speaks lies and deception, shall not any more prevail in imprisoning the minds of His people; plainly declaring the facts that if any man believes that Jesus died for him, then Christ must have died for the church in him and not the building in which we attend fellowship, meetings, or weekend services! Remember, God did not send His Son to come to die for a brick structure, an erected edifice, or a storefront church. Jesus, the Bible tells us, died for the sheep and not the sheepfold.

The sheep, the elects of God, called God's people, shall overcome, they will open their mouths and proclaim liberty to those who are held captive, and they with those who hear them shall become free too. *"Take heed unto thyself, and unto the doctrine; continue in them: for in doing this thou shalt both save thyself, and them that hear thee" (1 Timothy 4:16).*

There are two sets of temples on the earth, one which has the spirit of truth in it, and the other the spirit of error. *"We are of God: he that knoweth God heareth us; he that is not of God heareth not us. Hereby know we the spirit of truth, and the spirit of error" (1 John 4:6).* The one with the spirit of truth, God and His Son make their home in and the other, Satan manipulates. These two temples each have a gate; one gate proclaims truth and sets people free, and the other gate proclaims lies and deception, bringing many into bondage. *"Ye are of your father the devil, and the lusts of your father ye will do. He was a murderer from the beginning, and abode not in the truth, because there is no truth in him. When he speaketh a lie, he speaketh of his own: for he is a liar, and the father of it" (John 8:44).*

Everyone's faith comes by hearing, and only those who are willing to hear what is proceeding out of their own gate than any other gate stand to benefit the outcome of their intent. In other words, it's quite impossible for anyone to have faith in the Lord without having faith in themselves; you can't exhibit what you don't have, knowing that you are only what you are to others because of what you possess on the inside. What I am saying is, you are a product of what you know. Therefore, it is important, very important, that we let Christ heal our hearts so we can be made free by the very words spoken out of our own mouths and that which come from our own hearts. Else, if we must depend on another, then it must be someone who is sent from God, Someone who might speak as the Oracle of God.

So now, I hope all fully understand what Christ meant when He made reference regarding the building of His church, and the gates of hell which shall not prevail against it. Now if I asked, how many realize that the church that He is to build, represents His Body? *"And he is the head of the body, the church: who is the beginning, the firstborn from the dead; that in all things he might have the preeminence. Who now rejoice in my sufferings for you, and fill up that which is behind of the afflictions of Christ in my flesh for his body's sake, which is the church" (Colossians 1:18, 24).*

Oh yes, we could take it even deeper, but for now, let everyone ponder what has been discussed in this message. Open your gate, proclaim the truth, and your mind will be made free; free forever.

I believe we haven't lost the focus of the exposition of hell, taking into account the truth that hell symbolically and literally is interpreted as GRAVE. Many have said that the scriptures have a sense of humor, and I very much agree it does. For example, the thief on the cross on death row was able to shut out the world, death, and sin, and cried out saying, Jesus *"when thou come in thy kingdom remember me."* And the Lord Christ without hesitation responded, *"Today you shall be with me in paradise."* Question, what and where is paradise? To answer this question, we need to know where Jesus was taken, on the day He was brought down from the cross. The grave, of course, you will say.

Likewise, the thief. If hell represents the grave, shall we not connive with the scripture today that the grave is paradise?

In the English word web dictionaries, the word "paradise," is a noun word, meaning, "any place of complete bliss, delight, and peace." Christianity explains it to be the abode of righteous souls after death. Yet, figuratively, and synonymously, "paradise," this word of Persian origin, is used in the Septuagint as the translation of Eden. It means " an orchard of pleasure and fruits," a garden or "pleasure ground," something like an English park. It is applied figuratively to the celestial dwelling of the righteous, in allusion to the Garden of Eden."*He that hath an ear, let him hear what the Spirit saith unto the churches; To him that overcometh will I give to eat of the tree of life, which is in the midst of the paradise of God" (Revelation 2:7).*

It has thus come into familiar use to denote both the garden and the heaven of the just by Smith's Bible Dictionary.

Hell is a form of paradise; a place of blissful rest. In other words, when men pass over to the yonder, he rests from all his troubles, fears, anxiety, and worries. This is why Job said, "O that thou wouldest hide me in the grave," except with the understanding that it is the only place where there can be true peace from the cruelty of unsaved humanity.

So, when many read the works of Jesus saying, *"Today you shall be with me in paradise,"* they immediately concluded that the thief is right on his way to heaven, but unfortunately, Jesus wasn't referring to the paradise of Revelation 2:7, but for the essence of clarity, let us look at plain reasoning. How can the thief go to the kingdom, when He that was promised the kingdom hasn't gone, but says, *"And if I go and I prepare a place for you, I will come again, and receive you unto myself; that where I am, there ye may be also. And wither I go ye know, and the way ye know. I am the way, the truth, and the life: no man cometh unto the Father, but by me"(John 14:3–6).* When Thomas asked Him how they should know the way, Jesus said, if I go, then and only will you as my disciple know, how to make it there not earlier than was stipulated.

The humor in this fact is that Jesus who owns the kingdom has not even gone in as yet, how then can the thief go in? In looking at the event that transpired of the death of Jesus Christ and after three days when He rose from the dead, Mary knew not who Jesus was after He rose from the sepulcher. How then can any man know how or by which way they should get to heaven or the kingdom, when Jesus Christ himself hasn't gone? When we read the account of His resurrection, it is evident that no one would have known where to go except Jesus revealed it unto them (John 20:1–19).

Again, see Acts 2:30–32, *"Therefore being a prophet, and knowing that God had sworn with an oath to him, that of the fruit of his loins, according to the flesh, he would raise up Christ to sit on his throne; He seeing this before spake of the resurrection of Christ, that his soul was not left in hell, neither his flesh did see corruption. This Jesus hath God raised up, whereof we all are witnesses."*

Obviously, it is clear that if He hasn't gone, no man would or can go. Those who propagate that the dead believers in Christ are already in heaven hold no truth, knowing that there is no GPS made that can navigate the pathways to heaven. The Lord reported in John 3:13 saying there is no man ascended into heaven, but He that came down from heaven.

May I at this point say, the next time you attend a funeral, and the priest presiding over the function declares to everyone that the dead corpse has ascended up into heaven walking in the street of gold, please stop such a priest and insist that the casket be reopened or broken, whichever is quicker to ascertain that the body is really gone, else, there is no proof that the thief on the cross that Jesus promised the kingdom ever took the lead, leaving Christ behind.

All the pastors that have been assigned with the responsibility to use their ministries to guide men and women to find their entrance to the kingdom are responsible for the destination of the souls that come in unto them. Meaning, whether be the dispensing of the truth or the establishment of a lie, men have been empowered to find the truth of the Lord Jesus Christ with their heart and soul, whether it be in mysteries, parables, or clear simplicity of the words of instructions. *"With him is strength and wisdom: the deceived and the deceiver are his"* (Job 12:16).

"But woe unto you, scribes and Pharisees, hypocrites! for ye shut up the kingdom of heaven against men: for ye neither go in yourselves, neither suffer ye them that are entering to go in. Woe unto you, scribes and Pharisees, hypocrites! for ye compass sea and land to make one proselyte, and when he is made, ye make him twofold more the child of hell than yourselves" (Matthew 23:13,15).

"This is the generation of them that seek him, that seek thy face, O Jacob. Selah. Lift up your heads, O ye gates; and be ye lift up, ye everlasting doors; and the King of glory shall come in" (Psalms 24:6–7). Lift up your head O ye gates that the King of Glory may come in. The gates referred to in this scripture are pastors. God commands pastors to lift up their heads. He requires that men of God lift up their headship in the ministry, in the work of God, and in their personal faith walk with the Lord.

The Lord has promised that the gates of hell shall not prevail over the church. In other words, the mouth of false preachers shall not be able to stop the very elects from reaching the kingdom reserved for them by the Lord, because you own the right to seek the truth by searching out where His work is on the earth. The Bible says if you seek Him early, you shall find Him. While some might enter through the narrow way that leadeth to life, some might end up with the broad way that leadeth unto destruction. *"Enter ye in at the strait gate: for wide is the gate, and broad is the way, that leadeth to destruction, and many there be which go in there at: Because strait is the gate, and narrow is the way, which leadeth unto life, and few there be that find it"* (Matthew 7:13–14).

So purely depending on how we allow God to lead us and not ourselves will cause us to witness if the gate of hell will prevail over us or not. For if the word of God preached to us is not yielding life, then we must have been preached a lie, and no lie or liar can enter or inherit the kingdom of God. As it is written in Proverbs 18:21, *"Death and life is in the power of the tongue,"* so you are either receiving life, or you inhabiting death, but thank God that the very elects cannot be deceived. *"For there shall arise false Christs, and false prophets, and shall shew great signs and wonders; insomuch that, if it were possible, they shall deceive the very elect" (Matthew 24:24).* For He promised that no man would ever be able to pluck the very chosen out of His hands. Isn't God wonderful! *"My sheep hear my voice, and I know them, and they follow me: And I give unto them eternal life; and they shall never perish, neither shall any man pluck them out of my hand. My Father, which gave them me, is greater than all; and no man is able to pluck them out of my Father's hand" (John 10:27–29).*

"But the fearful, and unbelieving, and the abominable, and murderers, and whoremongers, and sorcerers, and idolaters, and all liars, shall have their part in the lake which burneth with fire and brimstone: which is the second death" (Revelation 21:8).

8

The Dead is Dead

In the dispensation of working as a believer, there is this understanding that the dead in Christ move out alive. Well, it is far from being the truth. There is no way the dead can move out alive when their change has not come. Having read the issue that there is no immortality of the soul, it's not possible for the dead to move out alive, or be in existence outside of the framework of the body. In the book of Ecclesiastes 12:7, *"Then shall the dust return to the earth as it was: and the spirit shall return unto God who gave it."* It is clear that the dead remain in the dust. Every living person that has existed would end up in the dust, except for those who are not destined to be dead before the return of the Lord Jesus Christ. Yes, the spirit returns to God who gave it because the spirit cannot die. If we all remember, the spirit talked about, "it's the breath of the Almighty," which he breathed upon man for him to become a living soul. *"And the LORD God formed man of the dust of the ground, and breathed into his nostrils the breath of life; and man became a living soul" (Genesis 2:7).* Therefore, without the breath, the structure of a man remains practically a pack of dust or clay. No one of course can hold the air, which God breathed upon the nostrils of man, showing that the air breathed upon man was not literal air, but a spirit.

In getting deep into the understanding of the breath of man as a spirit, it will be interesting to note that when the disciples were to be filled with the Holy Spirit in the upper room, there was the presence of two major elements, one of which was the wind. *"And suddenly there came a sound from heaven as of a rushing mighty wind, and it filled all the house where they were sitting" (Acts 2:2)*. Therefore, either literally or spiritually, the wind is a vital part of the spirit of God. As that air, being the spirit of God enters into man, man becomes a living soul. Jesus said in John 3:6, *"that when a man is born of flesh, he is of the flesh, and when man is born of the spirit, he is of the spirit,"* showing us also that for a man to take on a level of spirituality, he must be impacted by the breath of God. God has to breathe upon us again!

Very many of us have underplayed a very important scripture in our Christian walk, neglecting the truth involved with such understanding. What am I talking about? The dry bones of Ezekiel, did they move out alive? If they did, then they would have not needed the breath, the wind called for by Ezekiel the prophet from the four corners of the earth to fall on the slain dry bones for them to become a living soul *(Ezekiel 37:9)*. In other words, for the dry bones of Ezekiel 37 to come alive, there was a necessity of commanding the wind to fall upon the dead dry bones, for God alone has that authority and power to give life by breath, to give life by the wind, to make alive a mere clay, by which today every mortal being can declare that they are a living soul by the reasoning of God's manifestation. So, without contradiction, the dead being dead without the breath should not be a mystery.

Hitherto, the dead man remains in the grave, as it was written in Ecclesiastes 3:20, *"All go unto one place; all are of the dust, and all turn to dust again."* The promise of God to humanity was after they have lived their probation on this earth, they will surely die, and return to the state of the dead. They remain in that state until the return of Christ. Job said that man's foundation is dust, and his tabernacle is of clay, therefore, they stand not the chance of the moth. *"The waters wear the stones: thou washest away the things which grow out of the dust of the earth; and thou destroyest the hope of man" (Job 14:19).*

As a matter of fact, the excellence of man goes away and they die without wisdom or knowledge of what comprises their existence. *"Doth not their excellency which is in them go away? They die, even without wisdom" (Job 4:21).* Job happened to be a man who took his time to comprehend his existence. He understood that man lived in this life as a hireling, who must work until he accomplishes his days. *"Man that is born of a woman is of few days, and full of trouble. He cometh forth like a flower, and is cut down: he fleeth also as a shadow, and continueth not. And dost thou open thine eyes upon such a one, and bringest me into judgment with thee? Who can bring a clean thing out of an unclean? not one. Seeing his days are determined, the number of his months are with thee, thou hast appointed his bounds that he cannot pass; Turn from him, that he may rest, till he shall accomplish, as a hireling, his day" (Job 14:1–6).*

It is important that we have the life of Christ within us, that we may avoid the life of crisis called judgment or tribulation, that's right ahead of the human age. Permit me to say that life without Christ is a life with insanity. As they say, to live in the wrong and know that you're in the wrong and want no correction is the beginning of insanity. In the book of John, we were made to know that God sent His Son into the world, that through Him the world might be saved and not be condemned. Yet many choose not to believe in His Son. Knowing that whosoever believeth not on His Son is condemned already, so are all those that are dead without Christ will remain in the dust without a restoration. *"For God sent not his Son into the world to condemn the world; but that the world through him might be saved. He that believeth on him is not condemned: but he that believeth not is condemned already, because he hath not believed in the name of the only begotten Son of God" (Joh 3:17–18).*

Now, to identify with the resurrection, the dead remain dead until Jesus shall call them from the grave and they that have done good shall come forth unto the resurrection of life, and those that have done evil unto the resurrection of damnation. And not until that happens, the dead remain in the state of being dead. *"And they shall be gathered together, as prisoners are gathered in the pit, and shall be shut up in the prison, and after many days shall they be visited" (Isaiah 24:22).* The only hope of resurrection is until God grants the breath or spirit, he took from them. *"Thou hidest thy face, they are troubled: thou takest away their breath, they die, and return to their dust" (Psalms 104:29).*

All the living know that they shall die if Christ delays His coming. All among men have the tendency of being dead, and when death ensues, no one remembers God, nor seek after salvation, neither do they have any more a reward for anything that is done underneath the sun, and neither will God show them any more wonder, nor will they be able to give God a celebrated praise.

"For the living know that they shall die: but the dead know not anything, neither have they any more a reward; for the memory of them is forgotten. Also, their love, and their hatred, and their envy, is now perished; neither have they any more a portion forever in anything that is done under the sun" (Ecclesiastes 9:5–6).

"Whatsoever thy hand findeth to do, do it with thy might; for there is no work, nor device, nor knowledge, nor wisdom, in the grave, whither thou goest" (Ecclesiastes 9:10).

"For in death there is no remembrance of thee: in the grave who shall give thee thanks?" (Psalms 6:5).

"Wilt thou shew wonders to the dead? shall the dead arise and praise thee? Selah. Shall thy lovingkindness be declared in the grave? or thy faithfulness in destruction?" (Psalms 88:10–11).

Though there is a myth that the dead do come to the party of the living and they appear to living relatives. Oh, if this were true, then all men would have been most comforted. While it might appear true that individuals have visitations of ghosts appearing to them, there is no biblical evidence of this fact. It is not farfetched, that the devil will perpetrate any act to lay deception in the pathway of unsuspecting souls. Especially with reference to the above scriptures, the dead live not again either physically, spiritually, or superstitiously, to associate with the living. The memory is forgotten, their hope perisheth, their knowledge vanisheth, the Bible says. If it be true that the dead do come back as ghosts, either friendly or evil ghosts, then the world would have been the world of both the living and the dead. This is why the living mourn their dead because they will never see them again until when they shall arise to obtain their reward. *"And I saw the dead, small and great, stand before God; and the books were opened: and another book was opened, which is the book of life: and the dead were judged out of those things which were written in the books, according to their works. And the sea gave up the dead which were in it; and death and hell delivered up the dead which were in them: and they were judged every man according to their works" (Revelation 20:12–13).* Only then will both the living and the dead stand again in company of one another.

9

The Weeping and Gnashing of Teeth

In the New Testament, there are seven passages that speak about the weeping and gnashing of teeth.

"And I say unto you, That many shall come from the east and west, and shall sit down with Abraham, and Isaac, and Jacob, in the kingdom of heaven. But the children of the kingdom shall be cast out into outer darkness: there shall be weeping and gnashing of teeth" (Matthew 8:11–12).

"The Son of man shall send forth his angels, and they shall gather out of his kingdom all things that offend, and them which do iniquity; And shall cast them into a furnace of fire: there shall be wailing and gnashing of teeth" (Matthew 13:41–42).

"And he saith unto him, Friend, how camest thou in hither not having a wedding garment? And he was speechless. Then said the king to the servants, Bind him hand and foot, and take him away, and cast him into outer darkness; there shall be weeping and gnashing of teeth" (Matthew 22:12–13).

"The lord of that servant shall come in a day when he looketh not for him, and in an hour that he is not aware of. And shall cut him asunder, and appoint him his portion with the hypocrites: there shall be weeping and gnashing of teeth" (Matthew 24:50–51).

"For unto everyone that hath shall be given, and he shall have abundance: but from him that hath not shall be taken away even that which he hath. And cast ye the unprofitable servant into outer darkness: there shall be weeping and gnashing of teeth" (Matthew 25:29–30).

"But he shall say, I tell you, I know you not whence ye are depart from me, all ye workers of iniquity. There shall be weeping and gnashing of teeth, when ye shall see Abraham, and Isaac, and Jacob, and all the prophets, in the kingdom of God, and you yourselves thrust out" (Luke 13:27–28).

Many have outrageously referred to these passages as doom's domain for sinners, signifying hell to be an inferno. But inevitably, none of these suggest punishment or torture, but remorse, regret, and unaccomplishment. To help us digest the argument of hell in relation to the phrase there shall be "weeping and gnashing of teeth," it will be helpful to consider once again the true understanding of hell. In Deuteronomy 32:22–24, *"For a fire is kindled in mine anger, and shall burn unto the lowest hell, and shall consume the earth with her increase, and set on fire the foundations of the mountains. I will heap mischiefs upon them; I will spend mine arrows upon them. They shall be burnt with hunger, and devoured with burning heat, and with bitter destruction: I will also send the teeth of beasts upon them, with the poison of serpents of the dust,"* the scripture equated the anger of God to hell. His anger is what will burn, not hell itself, but the anger of God the Father is what is going to burn unrepented sinners until they become consumed in hell, which is the grave. Out of the seven scriptures mentioned above, it is interesting to declare that only two of them speak about the "furnace of fire." While these two scriptures establish hell as a burning place, it will be noteworthy to say that Christ made those statements in the tone of a parable. The reason being that, Jesus spake not unto the people except in parable. *"All these things spake Jesus unto the multitude in parables; and without a parable spake he not unto them: That it might be fulfilled which was spoken by the prophet, saying, I will open my mouth in parables; I will utter things which have been kept secret from the foundation of the world" (Matthew 13:34–35).* At a point in time, even the disciples wondered why He spake so much in parable to the people; they couldn't understand it. They wanted to know and out of curiosity they were compelled to ask the Master in Matthew 13:10 saying, *"Why do you speak to the multitude in parable and not in plain language?"* The response of the Lord is what gave light to the disciples of that day.

Today, many still haven't comprehended that teaching of Christ, because of the parabolic application. Whether it be the saints of old or the believers of today, the word of Jesus Christ remains a mystery to those who are not called, nor chosen, to appreciate the knowledge of truth. *"And the disciples came, and said unto him, Why speakest thou unto them in parables? He answered and said unto them, Because it is given unto you to know the mysteries of the kingdom of heaven, but to them it is not given" (Matthew 13:10–11).*

Therefore, both scriptures of Matthew 13:41–42, *"The Son of man shall send forth his angels, and they shall gather out of his kingdom all things that offend, and them which do iniquity; And shall cast them into a furnace of fire: there shall be wailing and gnashing of teeth,"* and Matthew 13:49–50, *"So shall it be at the end of the world: the angels shall come forth, and sever the wicked from among the just, And shall cast them into the furnace of fire: there shall be wailing and gnashing of teeth,"* suggest that the wicked being thrust into a burning furnace was only a parabolic language, expressing the torture of the wicked because of their unrepented heart. According to Deuteronomy 32:22–24, *"For the fire that will kindled in God's anger, that shall burn unto the lowest hell, and consume the earth with her increase, and set on fire the foundations of the mountains. Simply means They shall be burnt with hunger, and devoured with burning heat, and with bitter destruction: And the teeth of beasts that will be set upon them, with the poison of serpents of the dust are all marks of bitter destruction. Mankind will see that the anger of God was a fury of hunger, burning heat, bitter destruction, the teeth of the beast and the poison of serpents of the dust."*

In Malachi, the proud and the wicked shall be as stubble in the oven of God's anger. *"For, behold, the day cometh, that shall burn as an oven; and all the proud, yea, and all that do wickedly, shall be stubble: and the day that cometh shall burn them up, saith the LORD of hosts, that it shall leave them neither root nor branch" (Malachi 4:1).*

Did you know that the anger of God that shall strike the earth, that shall burn like a wrath with the fury of hunger was also prophesied in Lamentations 4:8–11? *"Their visage is blacker than a coal; they are not known in the streets: their skin cleaveth to their bones; it is withered, it is become like a stick. They that be slain with the sword are better than they that be slain with hunger: for this pine away, stricken through for want of the fruits of the field. The hands of the pitiful women have sodden their own children: they were their meat in the destruction of the daughter of my people. The LORD hath accomplished his fury; he hath poured out his fierce anger, and hath kindled a fire in Zion, and it hath devoured the foundations thereof."* Who in this state of being will not weep and gnash their teeth? Who can have the joy of comeliness? Who can stand in that day when the earth shall shake and tremble, and the foundation thereof be shaken? Brethren, something is going to happen, let us not delay in seeking our salvation with fear and trembling, or rather work out our salvation with fear and trembling.

Most Christians, who must have paid close attention to all of the relative scriptures, must realize that the weeping and gnashing of teeth is in relation to those who are unbelieving believers. Those who were in a proper church setting, face to face with the daily use of the scriptures, yet chose not to live or abide by the knowledge of truth. They chose to be unregenerated, thereby, counting themselves not worthy of the saving grace of God or the much-emphasized kingdom of our Lord and Savior Jesus Christ. These men and women did the Lord typify in the scripture to be wicked and needed to be cast out into outer darkness.

"And I say unto you, That many shall come from the east and west, and shall sit down with Abraham, and Isaac, and Jacob, in the kingdom

THE WEEPING AND GNASHING OF TEETH

of heaven. But the children of the kingdom shall be cast out into outer darkness: there shall be weeping and gnashing of teeth" (Matthew 8:11–12).

"And he saith unto him, Friend, how camest thou in hither not having a wedding garment? And he was speechless. Then said the king to the servants, bind him hand and foot, and take him away, and cast him into outer darkness; there shall be weeping and gnashing of teeth" (Matthew 22:12–13).

"For unto everyone that hath shall be given, and he shall have abundance: but from him that hath not shall be taken away even that which he hath. And cast ye the unprofitable servant into outer darkness: there shall be weeping and gnashing of teeth" (Matthew 25:29–30).

"But he shall say, I tell you, I know you not whence ye are depart from me, all ye workers of iniquity. There shall be weeping and gnashing of teeth, when ye shall see Abraham, and Isaac, and Jacob, and all the prophets, in the kingdom of God, and you yourselves thrust out" (Luke 13:27–28).

The term "outer" can be related to or considered exclusion. Meaning, total denial of a place in the kingdom or complete rejection due to a person's unsaved condition.

Permit me to say, although the term "outer darkness" is found in four passages of the scriptures, there are other scriptures that describe hell as a place of terrible darkness. *"Raging waves of the sea, foaming out their own shame; wandering stars, to whom is reserved the blackness of darkness forever" (Jude 1:13). "These are wells without water, clouds that are carried with a tempest; to whom the mist of darkness is reserved for ever" (2 Peter 2:17).*

So, in considering the scriptures, those that are to be cast out into outer darkness are the children of Israel who by birth or by inheritance neglected their God-given opportunity of redemption. While the Gentile believers who being the seed of Abraham by faith, are able to enter into the kingdom by grace, the outer darkness that the children of Israel and the unbelieving believers shall be thrown out into will be torment or torture, regret, confusion, pestilence, disease, fear, and sometimes even death. But to the righteous and the faithful, God will bring light and life. *"Therefore judge nothing before the time, until the Lord come, who both will bring to light the hidden things of darkness, and will make manifest the counsels of the hearts: and then shall every man have praise of God"* (1 Corinthians 4:5).

The Lord commanded us through the ministry of Apostle Paul to walk with them that are without. Thereby saying that those who are without, are those that have no God nor virtue of salvation. *"That ye may walk honestly toward them that are without, and that ye may have lack of nothing"* (1 Thessalonians 4:12). *"Blessed are they that do his commandments, that they may have right to the tree of life, and may enter in through the gates into the city. For without are dogs, and sorcerers, and whoremongers, and murderers, and idolaters, and whosoever loveth and maketh a lie"* (Revelation 22:14–15).

The Lord promised His believers that they will never be left in outer darkness. *"Giving thanks unto the Father, which hath made us meet to be partakers of the inheritance of the saints in light: Who hath delivered us from the power of darkness, and hath translated us into the kingdom of his dear Son"* (Colossians 1:12–13).

But rather, He giveth a light that will sustain them until the end. *"But ye, brethren, are not in darkness, that that day should overtake you as a thief. Ye are all the children of light, and the children of the day: we are not of the night, nor of darkness"* (1 Thessalonians 5:4–5).

"For I speak to you Gentiles, inasmuch as I am the apostle of the Gentiles, I magnify mine office: If by any means I may provoke to emulation them which are my flesh, and might save some of them" (Romans 11:13–14).

He promised to open their eyes and to turn them from darkness to light. *"To open their eyes, and to turn them from darkness to light, and from the power of Satan unto God, that they may receive forgiveness of sins, and inheritance among them which are sanctified by faith that is in me"* (Acts 26:18).

"But ye are a chosen generation, a royal priesthood, an holy nation, a peculiar people; that ye should shew forth the praises of him who hath called you out of darkness into his marvelous light" (1 Peter 2:9).

"Then spake Jesus again unto them, saying, I am the light of the world: he that followeth me shall not walk in darkness, but shall have the light of life" (John 8:12).

Therefore, the gnashing of teeth does not significantly mean torture or anguish in the burning hell, but anger or sorrow because of failure of penitence. We will see when the Jews were furious about the sayings of Stephen. They hated the message that Stephen had to confront them with the need of a conversion. See their reaction in Acts 7:54, *"When they heard these things, they were cut to the heart, and they gnashed on him with their teeth."* These go to explain that weeping and gnashing represent anger and rage when people failed their expected positions in this life. So, if Jesus does come today, there will be many who will consider Him unfair when He shall apportion their rewards. When they see that rapture eludes them and their place and their thoughts were not up to expectation, they will stand out with fury and wrath, while carrying a burden of sorrow because of their failure. There shall be weeping and gnashing of teeth in retaliation to God or man.

CONCLUSION

Why would we want to wrest the scriptures to no reputation nor to the savings of our soul, adding to the word of God which is literally forbidden? Let us, with one heart, seek the truth of the word of God so that we don't live only to have eternity to regret, but a place to enter into His rest. For He has said, *"Ye shall know the truth and the truth shall make you free."* AMEN.

www.ingramcontent.com/pod-product-compliance
Lightning Source LLC
LaVergne TN
LVHW092053060526
838201LV00047B/1366